SECRET GARDENS OF

HOLLYWOOD

AND PRIVATE OASES IN LOS ANGELES

SECRET GARDENS OF

HOLLYWOOD

AND PRIVATE OASES IN LOS ANGELES

Erica Lennard

TEXT BY Adele Cygelman

INTRODUCTION BY Robert Smaus

UNIVERSE

FIRST PUBLISHED IN THE UNITED STATES OF AMERICA IN 2003 BY

UNIVERSE PUBLISHING

A Division of Rizzoli International Publications, Inc.
300 Park Avenue South
New York, NY 10010

2003   2004   2005   2006   2007   /   10   9   8   7   6   5   4   3   2   1

Printed in China
DESIGN BY Sara E. Stemen

Library of Congress Control Number: 2002115774
ISBN 0-7893-0881-9

I am grateful to everyone who shared their gardens and their love of gardening with us, and to the friends who helped us to unearth these treasures. A special thanks to my friend Laurie Frank, without whom this book would not have been possible: Laurie made me fall in love with Los Angeles; she introduced us to the extraordinary gardeners Patrick Bauchau and Mijanou Bardot; she acquainted us with the many amazing gardeners in this book.

Thanks also to Robert Dyer, Julie Milligan, Nonna Summers, and Susan Zsigmond. I am grateful to Jeff Nemeroff for introducing me to Adele, who has accompanied me on this journey.

A special thanks to our editor, Alex Tart, to my agent, Helen Pratt, and to our designer, Sara Stemen. Finally, thanks to my husband, Denis Colomb, for sharing his passion for gardening with me. Maybe one day we will make our own garden...

—ERICA LENNARD

A paragraph in the *Western Garden Book* (Sunset Books), my bible for this project, says it all—"Palms and Pools: Perfect Partners." I love palm trees. To me, they say "Los Angeles." I couldn't imagine living without them. In this town, it helps that they look good by day and at night.

I thank each gardener featured in this book. They have trained my eye to look beyond the palms and appreciate the diversity of the city's landscape.

Some common themes emerged: Everyone named Lotusland in Santa Barbara and the succulent gardens at the Huntington in San Marino as their inspirations. Everyone had a statue of Buddha somewhere. All women mentioned the urge at age forty to get their hands into dirt. And everyone thought of their garden as a retreat, a sanctuary, a place that transports them into a different world.

My thanks to Erica for inviting me on this journey; to Alex Tart and Universe Publishing; and to Bob and Annie for giving me my own little piece of paradise.

—ADELE CYGELMAN

OPPOSITE: Hollywood meets the Mediterranean in a corner of Gloria Swanson's former garden, now owned by designer Martyn Lawrence-Bullard.

It should come as no surprise that the gardens of Hollywood are nearly as fanciful as the films produced here, and equally as varied. It would seem odd if they were not. The same vision that animates movies enlivens the gardens of those who are even remotely connected.

You don't have to actually work in the movies to be influenced by them. Most who live in the vicinity of Hollywood—and remember that Hollywood is not a separate town but a vibrant corner of the city of Los Angeles—are here because they like the spirit and soul of the place. It's creative, inventive—even daring—and highly individualistic, as are its gardens. No garden style dominates here; there is no certain look that must be followed. It is possible to find almost any garden style or setting in Hollywood or its hills.

The movies of Hollywood are expert at making themselves seem to be somewhere else: that quaint New England village is actually on a backlot in Hollywood (or nearby Culver City or Universal City); that Parisian café is on a studio soundstage, and so on. In like manner, many gardens in this part of town look as if they are somewhere else—in Hawaii, Tuscany or the Cotswolds—partly because, a long time ago, early gentlemen farmers discovered that just about anything grows in Hollywood.

In the late 1880s, just off what was to become Hollywood Boulevard, Jacob Miller found he could grow the exotic avocado trees he had imported from Guatemala, though he had less success with the coffee trees he brought back. Growing nearby were apricots and guavas, grapes and melons, olives and oranges, and even bananas. Daeida Wilcox grew figs on her ranch before her husband Harvey subdivided part of the tract, calling it Hollywood. It was Daeida's suggestion. She had heard someone talking about a country estate in Illinois, that was named Hollywood

Far from Hollywood, but still under the spell of the fantasy garden, actors Brigitte Helm and Gustav Frohlich cavort amid waterfalls and peacocks on the set of Fritz Lang's masterpiece, *Metropolis*, 1926.

because it was surrounded by holly trees. Harvey Wilcox tried repeatedly to grow traditional English holly on his property, only to discover that it is one of those plants that doesn't grow terribly well in Southern California, though other kinds of holly do quite nicely.

As tracts replaced farms, weekend gardeners continued the adventure—finding what would grow in this new, untested climate. Early garden experimenters such as Dr. Francesco Franceschi in Santa Barbara devoted their lives to seeing just what he could get away with, introducing hundreds of new plants from exotic locales. Gardeners found that winter cold presented no constraints to gardening in the Southland and the word "hardy" hardly had any meaning. Favorite plants were grown side by side with little regard for climate or even culture.

Being able to grow almost anything had a huge impact on what gardens should or could look like—the idea that gardens *should* look a certain way gave way to an almost anything-goes free-for-all. This has inexorably led to today's amazing variety of garden types. If you can think it, you can probably plant it. No matter how fantastic it may seem, it is probably doable. Combine this with the free-thinking crowd around Hollywood, and you're going to get some very inventive gardens.

Painter Paul De Longpré planted such a garden way back in the 1890s, quickly becoming more famous for his garden of bold and flowery strokes—which he opened to the public—than for his colorful paintings and prints. He had traded three paintings for three acres on the corner of Hollywood Boulevard and Cahuenga and it became one of Los Angeles's first tourist attractions. When a train line was built from downtown Los Angeles to Hollywood, it ended at the entrance to his garden.

On the other side of town, in Pasadena, brewer Adolphus Busch came from St. Louis and built himself a garden on thirty acres near the Arroyo Seco. The garden had fourteen miles of trails that led visitors to little lands peopled with characters from Grimm's fairy tales and exquisitely planted in a naturalistic fashion by a talented Scotsman. It too became a crowd pleaser, open to the public for fourteen years and an obvious harbinger of things to come, including the fanciful Disney parks. Visitors, of course, went home and tried to do the same thing in their gardens, if on a more modest scale.

Landscapes like De Longpré's and Busch's became gardens that were also entertainment, which meshed nicely with another form of entertainment taking root in the Southland. The same good weather that allowed one to grow anything also allowed filming outdoors in any season. That's how Hollywood, the industry, was born. Early motion picture moguls built palatial homes in the hills of Hollywood and landscaped them lavishly. During the 1920s and 1930s, in what is called the golden age of gardens (as well as movies), the most talented landscape architects worked here—people like Edward Huntsman-Trout, Lockwood de Forest, A. E. Hanson, and Florence Yoch. These designers were considered innovators and experimenters.

Florence Yoch, with partner Lucille Council, actually designed sets for movies, the best remembered of which was *Gone with the Wind*. Her gardens, however, were anything but setlike, being quite substantial and elegant, so it is a bit surprising that so few survive today, even given this town's penchant for knocking things down and starting fresh.

A few celebrities are quite capable of creating their own gardens, the most famous of which is Lotusland, now administered by a foundation and open to the public on a limited basis.

OPPOSITE: Closer to home, in a photograph from 1918, director King Vidor clips wisteria while his wife, actress Florence Vidor, holds a basket of calla lilies. PHOTOGRAPH COURTESY OF THE KOBAL COLLECTION/NELSON EVANS

Stars Veronica Lake and Ronald Colman were captured at home in distinctly unglamorous poses, she with her hands in the dirt (taken in 1942), he mowing the lawn (in 1937). VERONICA LAKE IMAGE COURTESY OF THE KOBAL COLLECTION/PARAMOUNT/MAL BULLOCH; RONALD COLMAN PHOTOGRAPH COURTESY OF THE KOBAL COLLECTION

Opera diva Ganna Walska, who had been fortunate enough to have been married to several very wealthy husbands, turned the forty-acre estate in Santa Barbara into a series of highly imaginative tableaus with lavish subtropical plantings. One of these featured a remarkable collection of rare succulents with paths and pools festooned in seashells; another was the first blue garden. Although done late in her life—a good generation before similar schemes began to show up in other gardens—she was paving new territory, so to speak, in this case with blue fescue grass and blue-gray succulent foliage. These flowed riverlike between plantings of squat blue palms, under a canopy of blue Atlas cedars and blue spruce. The path that wound though this misty garden was lined with the blue glass slag left over from the production of Coca-Cola bottles. No one had thought of a blue garden before.

As this elegant era of estate gardens came to a close, smaller gardens got their turn. Californians had discovered that they could be outdoors on almost any day of the year and in the 1950s and 1960s landscape architects such as Garrett Eckbo were making outdoor living possible by designing gardens that were a lot like rooms. There were cool places to sit in the striped shade of lath, or warm patios for lounging. They added places to cook or pot plants, and provided for privacy. In California, gardens are not generally out in the open but are surrounded by greenery or tall fences (eight feet is allowed in Los Angeles), which makes them very private places.

Some suspect that we are now in our second golden age of garden making, as the twenty-five gardens in this book will suggest. This time around, gardens are even more varied and diverse. Recent emigrants to Hollywood and Los Angeles have brought new material with them—from a great many distinct places and cultures—which has captured the imaginations of gardeners and garden makers.

Southland designers such as Christine Rosmini, Isabelle Green, Nancy Goslee Power, Mia Lehrer, and Jay Griffith have noticeably changed the look of gardens in recent years, grabbing the attention of the garden world. But they are the mere tip of a green iceberg. There are hundreds of designers at work and thousands of amateurs, some with the talent to become designers themselves (a few have actually made that jump). Photographer Erica Lennard, herself a resident of Hollywood with a remarkable garden, said she simply had to stop shooting at twenty-five gardens. There had to be an end to the book.

She says these were chosen because each was quite different from the other, so much so that she felt as though she had taken a trip around the world while viewing them, even though they are all clustered in that one small corner loosely called Hollywood. So please, join us for a peek over the fence at some of our neighbors' most remarkable gardens.

—ROBERT SMAUS

[MEDITERRANEAN]

Behind every good set is a production designer, someone who can conjure an entire world for an imaginary character to inhabit onscreen. "My job is to get inside a character's head and figure out what makes him or her tick," says production designer Barbara Drake, whose credits include *Full Metal Jacket*, *Diggstown*, and *Home for the Holidays*. "In the film business you create a fantasy that has to look like reality. Here, I had no director and I could write my own script."

"Here" is a 1930s Spanish-style house in the heart of Los Angeles that glows inside and out with vibrant colors. Five years ago it was a rundown house on a narrow, deep lot. Up front was a tired lawn. In back were cracked concrete floors, a brick patio with a corrugated plastic roof, and a garage with peeling plaster walls. Giant ficus trees blocked the sun and the view of palm trees behind the house.

The moment Drake and her partner Peter Huck saw the property, she knew exactly what she wanted—a secret, mysterious, holistic garden. She also knew from her travels that she would install an Arabian-inspired inner courtyard with a fountain.

Drake is used to the speed of film sets—put up a wall, change your mind, move it, tear it down. "I have no fear of change," she says. "I ripped the house and the garden apart at the same time because they needed to be treated as one entity." At the same time that she was tearing out the interiors, Drake was removing the tired lawn and replacing it with succulents and herbs—mint, oregano, thyme, and rosemary. "I wanted drought-tolerant and healing plants that smell wonderful and that we could cook with," she says.

Walls, fences, and garage were all treated as a backdrop canvas and painted in a pale pistachio green, mixed from a piece of glazed pottery she found in Morocco. Doors, window frames, and the reflecting pool sport a

"I love lap pools, they're so geometric," says Barbara Drake. She credits Mexican architect Luis Barragán for inspiring the back garden's startling combination of a soothing pistachio green with a striking cobalt blue.

3

spectacular shade of cobalt blue called azul anil. The concrete floor in the rear was painted like tiles that remind Drake of a De Chirico painting. "I move the plants around like giant chess pieces."

The front entrance courtyard, with its eight-sided Andalusian fountain and deep banquettes meant for reclining, sets the stage for a Mediterranean fantasy. "You never know where a camera will be on a film set, and the garden is structured the same way," Drake says. "I tried to use every inch to the max. I have no favorite spots; wherever you sit, there's something different to look at.

"The garden is all about shape, space, and color and how you work it all together to form designs," Drake adds. Her main source of inspiration was Mexican architect Luis Barragán—his use of water structures and blocks of color, and way of manipulating light through a space. Everything else she absorbed by osmosis through travels to Mexico, India, Africa, Greece, and Morocco. "I'm drawn to the surreal, the dramatic, and the visually strong. I love the play of light and shadow."

She planted organic produce—arugula, salad lettuces, beets—and put in Mexican sage and fuchsia to attract hummingbirds. Then she added roses, jasmine, geraniums, bougainvillea, and citrus trees (orange, lime, lemons) for color and fragrance. The rosemary, lavender, and plumbago are all clipped and sculpted. "I like creating shapes and believe in controlled growth," Drake says. "Plants respond to being looked after." Cactus and succulents, especially aloe, became strong sculptural elements in their own right.

It's been a long and winding road from northern England, where she was born, via Kenya, where she lived as a child, to Los Angeles. Drake headed to Los Angeles ten years ago and felt an immediate kinship with the city's multiethnic mix and geographic diversity. "Coming to Los Angeles meant I was able to rid myself of the constrictions of England's rigid class system," she says. "Living away from your own society frees you, particularly here. I was finally able to cut the umbilical cord to my roots and let myself sail free."

"A courtyard with a fountain seems to touch deep in everyone's soul," Drake says. "It creates a feeling of well being and of protection. You're in the sun and protected from it. It muffles street sounds and transports you to another place. You can leave the cares and craziness of the city behind. It's a space to dream."

The reflecting pool mirrors the width of the corridor inside the house, thus allowing the eye to continue outdoors with no sense of interruption. "I'm very influenced by the environment and how we impact it. I use no chemicals or sprays and do minimal watering," says Drake, who keeps her rosemary and lavender clipped and uses succulents as sculpture in their own right.

LAURA MORTON AND JEFF DUNAS

Jeff Dunas is a photographer whose portraits are widely published in magazines and books (*American Pictures*, *State of the Blues*). Laura Morton is a jewelry designer who is slowly making the transition into garden design. Their home serves each a purpose: for Dunas, the garden is the ideal backdrop for his portrait sessions; for Morton, it is where she can put her ideas into practice.

A Greek architect built the house in 1921 as an earthquake prototype. It is solid concrete with sixteen-inch, steel-reinforced walls. Frank Gehry added a photo studio in 1981 that is in keeping with the Mediterranean motif—whitewashed walls and a flat roof. Depending on which way Dunas points his lens, the location could be North Africa or a Greek island. Dunas has studied the movement of light so minutely since they moved in, in 1994, that he knows precisely where and when to pose his subjects to get the best results. "The house makes me look like a genius," he says. He also installed all the lights and made sure that all light sources were hidden—there are no visible wall outlets or power sockets. There is nothing to break the illusion that this is Mykonos or Morocco.

The garden is Laura Morton's realm. Her original concept was to create a Japanese garden with a copper and bamboo teahouse, but that didn't work mainly because the house has few windows and doesn't overlook the garden—the garden is a whole other world, and there was no way to connect the Greek and Japanese aesthetics. And the old deck was down in the full sun while the garden area was in the shade. "When we finished decorating the interiors, we realized we liked Moroccan gardens," says Morton. They also realized that the garden and deck should be switched around—now the deck is in the shade and the garden gets full sun. In addition, they tore out the "horrendous 1970s pool" and brick patio, and put in flagstone.

~~~~~~

In the Mediterranean garden of landscape and jewelry designer Laura Morton and photographer Jeff Dunas, a giant wire dragonfly, one of Morton's creations, hovers over a rectangular water fountain that is covered with Moroccan tile.

Maintaining the Moroccan fantasy is the raised deck with its gas fire pit, lanterns, and deep banquettes covered with pillows. Morton lined the steps with cans of Greek olive oil filled with succulents.

The garden is dreamy and practical at the same time.
An incense burner evokes the Middle East while a row of
podocarpus down one side of the newly reconfigured pool
gives much-needed privacy.

The garden is now a Mediterranean melting pot—Moroccan doors, Tunisian pots, Greek olive oil and feta cans filled with succulents, and Marrakesh and Fez tile. The fantasy of Arabian nights plays out on the Moroccan deck with its deep banquettes and pillows. At night the gas fire pit "burns raging blue, like electricity," says Dunas. Both the octagonal fire pit and the rectangular water fountain at the other end of the pool were based on Islamic design principles. To one side of the deck is a tea garden where Morton has planted jasmine, eight kinds of mint, rose hip, and lemon verbena.

Morton has created a whimsical and spiritual place. The front steps were painted blue to look like flowing water and the front was planted with succulents that resemble an underwater fantasy of sea anemones and shells waving in the wind; it is bordered with rosemary. Her garden jewelry consists of wire dragonflies wrapped in the banana tree, pots filled with shells and pebbles, and a giant wind chime she made out of bamboo. Plants that attract hummingbirds were brought in. Succulents were potted to look like flower arrangements. "I like to work with a palette of two to three colors and different textures to create depth," she says. Down in the true garden, the flagstone disintegrates into pebbles, which gives the effect of a running river. Even the grout around the flagstone was inlaid with shells and glass. There is a row of podocarpus down the side. ("It's my favorite tree—ferny, leafy, shaggy, and tufty," she says.) Next to these are fruit trees—figs, apples, lemons, and loquats. A wisteria trailing over a trellis leads into the Asian garden at the side of the house, the one area that is in full view of the kitchen windows. There, all is dark and sensual, and in deep shade, and it's where Morton has indulged her "midnight witching hour" side: the rich burgundy of a Japanese maple; black bamboo; a Chinese opium bed, and magenta, purple, and brown plants growing out of chair seats. After she spent five years observing where their two dogs ran, Morton built hidden dog paths.

"I studied landscape architecture and horticulture, but I didn't want to sit at a desk drafting," says Morton, who is still taking courses at the Arboretum. "Landscape architecture is for freeway ramps and acres of grading, but a garden is an intimate thing. Our garden reveals and conceals."

Dunas uses elements in the garden as a backdrop for his portrait shoots. *OPPOSITE:* Morton likes to work with a limited palette of two to three colors and with a variety of materials to create layers. A mirror on the wall reflects her editing. *ABOVE:* Her jewelry for the garden includes amethyst geodes, glass balls, and minerals draped from a banana tree.

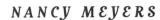

NANCY MEYERS

Every film that Nancy Meyers has written, produced or directed over the past twenty years has a common thread—a focus on females.

From *Private Benjamin* to *Baby Boom* to *What Women Want*, Meyers has made films about the average woman who struggles with career, babies, and family but who is still smart, funny, independent, and multilayered—women who operate firmly outside of the cliché box.

When landscape designer Mia Lehrer was brought in about four years ago, Meyers was in the process of creating a Mediterranean fantasy. "I thought that if you are doing a stage set, you might as well take it all the way," says Lehrer, who over the past two decades has established one of the top landscape design practices in Los Angeles. She set to work sketching a concept for the front and back that was her immediate response to the French/Italian farmhouse. Lehrer envisioned a scenario where the house had been carved out of an old olive grove, with ancient olive trees and irises spotted around as though they had been there forever—an imagined fantasy of grandma's house in Provence or Tuscany. "I felt very strongly about this idea, and usually my first instincts are right," she says.

The entire lot was dirt. Lehrer immediately put in a driveway of asphalt covered in gravel. Up some stairs on a wide terrace in front of the house, she put in a grove of olive trees interspersed with irises. A layer of gravel covers the terrace and connects it with the driveway. Pockets of rooms were created: a small formal parterre outside the living room; a terrace framed by white roses mixed with apple trees outside the dining room; and a lawn shaded by a pepper tree for having afternoon tea or lemonade.

Since the house has French doors that open onto the front and back gardens, she gave the two areas consistency with olive trees on both sides

A classic Mediterranean palette of olive trees, lavender, and white roses rises in front of Nancy Meyers's gracious Mediterranean house.

17

and the use of Mediterranean plant materials. A languid softness pervades the back garden, which has a wide expanse of lawn. Lehrer softened the colonnade outside the living room and office with vines that creep up and around the ceiling, rare China doll plants draped elegantly in pots, and an antique plant placed on an axis with the living room door.

"Personalities do come across in a garden," Lehrer says. "For Nancy it was all about beauty, aesthetics, and a very peaceful feeling—she didn't want it to be a backyard in Los Angeles. This garden is meant to put you in another world."

A small grove of crepe myrtles underplanted with *campanula* (bellflower), sycamore, and sweet olives add scent and flowers. A bank of rosemary leads up to the oval swimming pool. Nearby is a vegetable garden with giant zucchini, lettuce, rhubarb, thyme, basil, and artichokes. A walkway leads to an area with giant pots, urns, and a fountain. Each element was meant to add a dimension of age.

"Creative people get to fantasize about what they want—and they get to live out that fantasy," says Lehrer.

ABOVE: Landscape designer Mia Lehrer put in an olive grove underlaid with gravel and a flagstone path that leads to the house.

RIGHT: Since the house has French doors that open to the front and back, Lehrer repeated the olive trees in back for consistency.

OVERLEAF: Symmetrical vegetable garden beds and a meadow of lavender.

KONSTANTIN KAKANIAS

It makes perfect sense that Konstantin Kakanias has alighted in the ballroom of Barbara Stanwyck's old estate in historic Whitley Heights, a hilly jumble of glorious 1920s architecture near the Hollywood Bowl. It is the perfect marriage of over-the-top glamour and larger-than-life personality.

"I was very excited when I moved here. I didn't know what effect the garden would have," says the gregarious artist, whose wanderings have led him from Athens to Paris, Cairo, and New York. Now that Los Angeles is home, he has put down some roots, but of course they are portable ones. The large terrace outside the ballroom is filled with roses, dahlias, jasmine, geraniums, papyrus, hydrangea, fuchsia, and miniature fruit trees—orange and lemon—all in pots. Pots remind him of Italian gardens (his favorite) and they suit the Mediterranean architecture of the house. Pots also suit his lifestyle. "It's a gypsy thing—I can take the pots and go."

On a practical level, the garden acts as an extension of the ballroom/studio/loft. "There is a space problem," Kakanias admits. "I keep the doors open all the time because I like the continuation of the inside to the outside." On a creative level, the garden is his anchor. "The garden is my soothing medicine," he says. When he was working on his book *Mrs. Tependris: The Contemporary Years* (Rizzoli, 2002)—a hilarious illustrated romp through the contemporary art scene through the eyes of his pointy-nosed alter ego—he was looking out at the garden. "It gave me tremendous positive energy."

The ebullient Kakanias operates purely by emotional response. "Life is dedicated to beauty. I love to be surrounded by beautiful gardens, whether it's a modest terrace or a pot on someone's table," he says. "I love

"Elegance, symmetry, and understated magnificence" is an apt description of an original tiled pool and terrace on the old Barbara Stanwyck estate in Whitley Heights, currently the domicile of artist Konstantin Kakanias.

each plant as if it were human, and plants do love you back. I love natural fragrance—I can never have enough. I adore the odor of datura, and the fact that it's a fatal drug fascinates me."

The citrus, dahlias, and roses remind him of his native Greece, and whenever he gets homesick, Kakanias returns to his house on the island of Paros. There, his garden has ancient olive trees, a natural spring that spills out of rocks, and dahlias that grow triple. He protests that he knows nothing about gardening, but in fact he has absorbed the influences of Versailles, Sissinghurst, and the Moghul gardens in Kashmir, as any artist would. "They are great lessons in elegance, symmetry, and understated magnificence," he says. "Villa Lante and Boboli Gardens in Italy are subtle, not grandiose.

"The biggest surprise is the effect the garden has had on me—the pleasure and the moments of happiness it has given me," Kakanias reflects. "In my next life, I'd like to be a tree. Maybe an oak, but any kind would do."

The terrace outside the Spanish Colonial–style ballroom gives Kakanias extra living space to eat, sketch, and entertain.

A self-professed nomad who loves gardens, Kakanias
has planted dahlias, dwarf orange and lemon trees, roses,
jasmine, and papyrus in pots so that his garden is fragrant
yet portable.

[R O M A N T I C]

When architect Lise Matthews was working on additions to a 1930s Colonial house in Brentwood, she asked Susan Lindsey if she was interested in doing a fluff-up job on the landscaping. Two years later, the garden Lindsey created for actors Mary Steenburgen and Ted Danson and their family has become a magical wonderland.

"There were some specifics—I wanted water and lots of whimsical things," says Steenburgen. "Ted wanted a flat lawn where he could play touch football. But the garden is more about feelings." Steenburgen also paints, "so I know that gardens are all about painting with plants," she says. "I love the color green and I wanted to see the true beauty of green against green, with fewer flowering plants. Susan really liked that concept."

But gardens are such personal places, so specific and passionate and meaningful, and so symbolic of life and family and memories, that up until now Steenburgen had had a hard time collaborating with anyone on her houses and gardens. "I had never met anyone who had understood exactly what I wanted," the actress says. "Susan was part interpreter, part translator."

Steenburgen would drop phrases—"fairies in the garden," or "secret part," or "tumbly"—and Lindsey would plant things to create that feeling. "A garden should take you somewhere else, it should connect you consciously to your environment," says Lindsey, who trained and worked as an architect before turning to landscape architecture in the early 1990s. "Each space in a garden should make people feel a certain way. It has to have energy, but it has to take you away from the life you lead."

Steenburgen wanted to evoke the verdant greens of her native Arkansas, the baby's breath and mosses that cover the ground, the woods. When she was married to actor Malcolm McDowall she spent a lot of

Mary Steenburgen's request for water and whimsy translated into a pond below her Colonial-style house that has stepping stones, is filled with koi, and is surrounded by antique animal statuary that the actress collects at flea markets.

29

time in England, and she also wanted to capture the tumultuous beauty of English gardens, with their wildness and surprises. She also wanted to pay tribute to people who have passed away. She plans to put in a massive serviceberry tree in honor of her former sister-in-law Lady Gloria Birkett; the roses are a tribute to her friend, the late actor and photographer Roddy McDowall.

The front garden is soft and magical. Shading the lawn is a giant *magnolia grandiflora*—Steenburgen imagines elves living in its roots. The lawn slopes gently down past bowers to a pond filled with koi that has become the couple's favorite spot. "I'm amazed at how attached to the koi I've become," Steenburgen says. "They eat out of my hand." Around the pond she has placed whimsical animal garden ornaments and planters that she finds at flea markets and antiques stores. "I'm always on the lookout for things," she says. "I love bringing back pieces from Arkansas because they are a reminder of home." Hummingbirds, butterflies, and dragonflies are drawn to the pond, as are blue herons in search of succulent koi.

In a reverse of the typical garden layout, the back is more formal and structured, with clipped box hedges and low brick walls. "It was a job of subtraction," says Lindsey, who reduced the amount of brick walls and fussy brickwork, and softened the area with a fountain lined with abalone shells, a swan fountain, clematis vines on the walls, and feathery acacia. "Things grow like mad here," Lindsey says. "The garden has the best karma."

"Susan is so excited about her work that it's contagious," says Steenburgen. "She brilliantly and gracefully made me feel that it was all my doing. But under her guidance, I learned so much." At the end of the project Lindsey presented the couple with a special book about their garden, a guide with a description of the plants and how they grow and when they flower. "It's one of the best gifts we have ever received," says Steenburgen.

Landscape architect Susan Lindsey translated Steenburgen's desire for "tumbly" plants and "secret parts" into a country garden of soft, rounded forms in white, lavender, and pink: Japanese iris, Japanese anemone, cestrum, polygonum, and coral, mulberry, and Chinese fringe trees.

ABOVE LEFT: A swan fountain from antiques dealer Barbara Israel. *ABOVE RIGHT:* The back garden is more stately and formal, with brickwork, acacia trees, and boxwood hedges. *OPPOSITE:* A glory bower leads down to the pond and garden bench. "We planted things that evoked childhood memories," says Lindsey. "Magnolias and camellias, drippy lavender. Everything has a cozy sensibility."

At first glance it resembles an overgrown jungle, a chaotic, tumbling jumble of plants one on top of another. On closer inspection, however, the garden that Nick Taggart and Laura Cooper have nurtured reveals itself as a carefully thought-out expression of their artistry.

"We came to this as artists, not as horticulturists or landscape designers," Cooper says. She teaches at Art Center College of Design and does exhibits for the garden design show at the Los Angeles County Arboretum; he teaches at Otis Art Institute. He has lived in the house for twenty-five years. She moved in fourteen years ago. Cooper vividly remembers her first impression. "The walk up seduced me," she says. "It was like something out of a children's fairy tale that spoke to me and said, 'Make me a garden.'"

Set up on a deep slope in East Los Angeles, with views across to the campanile at Forest Lawn cemetery, the garden starts at street level with coils of cacti, which take the place of the more traditional hedge, and tangles of pepper trees, which are found at California's old missions.

"I wanted everything tall, and I wanted to be dwarfed, like Alice," Cooper says. "I tend to cram things in. There is no bare ground—I didn't want to see dirt. Now it's about editing and structure." As befits artists, palette dictates plant choice. "We go for color first, then form, and then variety of texture," says Taggart. "But there is no master plan, it just develops organically." They aren't purists and have put in a wide range of plants—Mediterranean, tropical, roses, "things that are tried and true and appropriate," says Cooper. The bottom is white and silver, the middle is a range of pinks, and the back, which gets most of the sun, has hotter yellows, orange, and reds.

Now that the couple has a new baby, they are putting a small grass area outside the kitchen. Close by is a coop for the Aracona and Buff

An organic mix of a giant cardoon, red flax, fig tree, and cactus are combined in Laura Cooper and Nick Taggart's garden in East Los Angeles. The artists see their garden as a counterpart to the house and a way to make the property seem larger by traveling through different areas.

ABOVE: "Gardens have a lot of drama at all levels," says Cooper. "So performances in an amphitheater seemed appropriate." The amphitheater was the last addition before the couple's baby arrived and has been the site of readings and music evenings.
OPPOSITE: The garden looks like a jungle but is actually an edited blend of the tried-and-true (roses, poppies, flax) with the unusual (agave attenuata, epazote, datura).

Orpington chickens and a compost heap. Their clay soil cracks like cement and requires lots of mulch, which is why they have a compost heap of chicken droppings and table scraps.

A window that opens out from the upstairs studio of the house started the whole notion of a treehouse and opening the house up to the garden. They have put in a new pond next to the house and created a series of outdoor rooms, and added formal structures that balance the wild garden—a couch near a fountain, and an arbor and table for outdoor dinners, an amphitheater for music performances and readings. "Places to sit are important," Cooper says. "I hold meetings and classes here—it's better than a classroom." Plants are intertwined everywhere: a fig tree is wrapped around a datura, roses are around an apricot tree, and plastic bracelets are twined around a mulberry tree.

"The garden has influenced our artwork. Now our art influences the garden," says Taggart, whose recent paintings of plants and insects magnify the subtle changes in the garden. "I'm becoming interested in plant forms and insects and the vignettes and drama going on." He waters the garden by hand every evening. "It's the best way to experience it and see what needs help."

They are inspired by other artists and sculptors like Ian Hamilton Finlay and Robert Irwin, who bring art into public spaces. "The one thing you have control over is your environment," says Cooper, "and this is our sanctuary. We feel like we're very far away. But we need to mix it up. The art world needs a dose of the physical world and the physical world needs more artistry."

The top of the garden next to the kitchen is the "hot spot" and is planted with red, yellow, and orange canna lilies, peppermint geraniums, euphorbia, and succulents. The clay soil benefits from the couple's chickens, who contribute to the compost heap.

We've got to get ourselves
Back to the garden

When Joni Mitchell first sang those words, she was referring to global consciousness. Now those same words also apply to Mitchell's own Los Angeles garden.

Although Mitchell has lived in the same house since 1974, until recently she has largely ignored her backyard. "The first ten years that I lived in the house, I was on the road or working on deadlines," says the singer/songwriter/artist whose latest album, *Travelogue*, features jazzy, throaty takes on some of her own classic songs. "I had no time to stop and smell the roses."

There were occasional forays into the garden. A landslide in 1976 ("the hills are hard brown sugar," she says) took out a lower orange grove but gave her room for a gazebo. A concrete strip is a memento from when she planned to have roller-skating parties. For the most part, though, Mitchell was content to let her gardener keep things going.

Then two years ago, when she lost three crown palms to blight—at the same time that the rainforest around her property in British Columbia was drying up— she decided to take a year off work and put her garden in order. "We have been fighting all kinds of blight since El Niño," she says. A pine tree had fallen through the roof. An avocado tree near the swimming pool sat in a puddle of chlorine from a burst pipe. A bougainvillea had turned spindly. "There were a lot of sick trees," she says. "I wanted to step outside and feel happy, not depressed because all these plants were dying."

Part Canadian, part Californian, and part student of comparative religion, Joni Mitchell gives voice to all her passions in her Bel-Air garden. She recently took a year off work to bring it back from neglect and blight. Kangaroo paw grows on either side of a red-tiled niche; center stage is a red-headed Tibetan Buddha, whom Mitchell calls a role model. "It's her disposition," she says. "When I go in the water I do kicks looking to her, and I swim better."

Her lushly planted collage—old camellias and gardenias, palms and ferns, fig trees, jacarandas and lilies—little resembles the all-white Mediterranean house that first greeted her in the 1970s. Now the house is muted in color—"the patina is just starting to get good"—and the garden is all gangly and full of weeds. "My favorite gardens are wild, not formal," says Mitchell. "I get more thrill out of the wild."

Mitchell is a flatlander, a child of the Canadian prairies and the first generation of her family to leave the farm. The blue grays/sage greens of Saskatchewan gardens are still the colors toward which she gravitates. Her own tiny childhood garden had *portulaca* (a succulent with waxy red flower and variegated leaves used as ground cover) and opium poppies; it's where she first fell in love with succulents.

"I plant freestyle. Nature picks the right spots," Mitchell says. "My gardener, Richard, left to his own devices, is a spacer—he would set plants up like picket fences. I'm a grouper." Together they planted crepe myrtles (her 90-year-old mother is named Myrtle) and silk trees. They pried away the honeysuckle that had overtaken the swing and "unburied" the jasmine that had been eaten up by a wisteria. They put in plants that attract butterflies, dragonflies, and hummingbirds. "Any flying, floating thing is auspicious, a joy bearer, a magical messenger," Mitchell says.

"It's hard to classify my garden—it doesn't have that American perfection," she adds. Brick edging and paths give it a "cottagey formality." She created vignettes in every corner with baker's racks, baskets, statues, and wallhangings that help break up the symmetry of the architecture. "It looked too new and boxy," she says. "It's nice when things get tumbly."

Mitchell is still adding to her garden—it is an eternal work in progress—but now she has turned her attention back to the recording studio. She dips into it when she needs reassurance or mental refreshment. "In every myth, we are the tenders of the gardens," she says. "Ancient cultures knew when to take and not, how to take and not, and they understood the custodianship of plants. My mother has always had a sustenance garden. She would always tell us that you don't need a psychiatrist if you have a garden. If I'm mad, I go pull weeds."

~~~~~~

TOP RIGHT: Branches fall and send pups out ("Nature thins itself out and adds things"), and become part of the "gangly, wild, weedy things" that Joni Mitchell loves. *BOTTOM RIGHT AND OPPOSITE*: Mitchell broke up the "boxy newness" of her house with vignettes, like the Grotto of Guadeloupe.

Mitchell inherited old gardenias and camellias and a white stucco house that she has gradually turned into a Spanish Colonial retreat. "Aromatics are the latest addition—jasmine and gardenias for pockets of scent," she says. "And we are putting aquatic plants around the well and fountain." There is a "wonderful crazy fig tree near the well—the fig is the tree of knowledge in folk art."

OPPOSITE: In the formal part, Mitchell and her gardener unearthed a swing that was overgrown with honeysuckle and anchored to the ground and put in brick paths and edging for what she calls "cottagey formality." *ABOVE LEFT:* Crepe myrtle, silk trees, jacaranda, and palms shade the residence. Mitchell says she is still drawn to "the weedy butterfly attractors and ditch-growing weeds of Saskatchewan." *ABOVE RIGHT:* "I learned as I planted," she says. "You can't put ferns under an oak—you can't put water lovers under dry lovers."

"I'm a mad rose person," Jamie Wolf admits cheerfully. In 1992, Wolf uprooted her family simply because she had run out of garden room. "We started looking for a house because I had planted roses on our roof and on a neighbor's lawn and became completely enamored with them," Wolf says. "I grew up in Connecticut and we didn't have roses, and I always wanted them. My mother didn't believe in flash or amplitude. I wanted the opposite."

Wolf now has about four hundred different roses—some in the ground, some in pots, and all labeled. She prefers the big, blowsy roses from the 1920s and 1930s—the ones that are full of fragrance and difficult to find.

The Wolfs moved from West Hollywood, near Sunset, to Beverly Hills, near Sunset. Their Tudor mansion was built in 1927 and had been home to Peter Falk and his first wife, a piano teacher who gave lessons at the house for years, then Polly Bergen and agent Freddie Fields, and then actor Macdonald Carey, who had four children. "Everyone played here," says Wolf. "We still get people coming by who used to play here."

When Wolf and her family moved in, the one-acre garden was composed of all red azaleas and yellow daisies. Working first with Judy Horton (see p. 84), then with her friend Katherine Spitz, and now with Hilary Bein, Wolf embarked on some intense gardening. "I would buy fifteen plants at a time and put them in the ground and they would all disappear," she says. "I had no concept of how many plants it would take to make an impact."

Roses, dahlias, and annuals make it a high-maintenance garden that requires constant organic spraying and deadheading. But Wolf—a jour-

Jamie Wolfe's passion for roses has taken over her mock-Tudor house in Beverly Hills. In the area of the garden that blooms from April through October is a peach-colored David Austin Leander rose (at left) with foxgloves and buddleia growing through the roses, true geraniums and, on the right, the Charlotte rose.

nalist who has contributed to *Los Angeles* magazine, *Harper's*, the *New Yorker*, and the *Wall Street Journal*—welcomes the switch to manual work. "Gardening is a relief from writing. It's so physical." Plus, she adds wryly, "The garden craze hits at forty—you can't control your kids anymore, so you control your garden."

Wolf now spends more time gardening than writing. "Maintenance is the enjoyable part—it puts you in touch with what's going on," she notes. "I like the physical hands-on, watching a bud turn into a flower. I'm a small-detail person rather than a big-picture person." Details include the ornaments—all her garden posts are copper and are topped with glass finials from old drawer pulls.

The garden is organized into specific "rooms," with each area a profusion of varieties and colors. "I like obscuring plants," says Wolf. "But negative space is also important." Camellias and a shady woodland are to the right. To the left is the "hot, gaudy" corner of bright orange astors mixed with hot raspberry roses, salvia, and phlox. Down one side is "The Farm," where she works with fewer colors—oranges and bright reds, a pomegranate tree. Around the pool is where Wolf has her annuals—zinnias and dahlias—for cutting. Every January she puts in fifteen hundred bulbs, thirty each of several varieties of tulips. "Planting bulbs is a complete indulgence, but I do it anyway."

The farm on the concrete path down the side of the house is her nursery. "I'm always trying out roses. I can always squeeze one more in," she says. "Theoretically you're sup-posed to weed them out, like a clothes closet." Wolf has even planted roses along the wall of the back alley—on the out-side. The back concrete driveway is a repository for roses in pots. "We didn't need a basketball court," she says.

The back is coastal redwoods and fruit trees (white Babcock peaches) and fifteen different kinds of sweet pea. "I want fragrance, especially in roses," says Wolf. "If they don't deliver, they go. It's the same with the sweet peas." She keeps dahlias in rotation with sweet peas (summer) and tulips (spring).

She turned a patch of grass in a corner into a secret garden and made a fountain out of art nouveau tile and an old sink and put in clematis, lilies, and shade-tolerant roses. It was designed to be a knot garden, and it will be one day, she says.

Wolf converted the laundry room in her house into a flower room. The walls and ceiling are covered with rose wall-paper. Vases, old and new, line the shelves of an antique cup-board. "I pick flowers practically every day. I listen to the radio and snip," Wolf says. "It's where I interact with the flowers. I'm a big flower arranger—I can spend ten hours a week doing it." Her office, which overlooks the garden, is filled with books by Louise Beebe Wilder, an American writer in the 1920s, and the self-deprecating humor of Vita Sackville-West, Eleanor Perenyi, and Katherine Angell White.

"I used to go out and look at other gardens, but I thought, 'Why am I here when I could be home working?'" she says. "I'm a bigger believer in tending. A garden is restorative and emotional. It balances out my organizational side."

Even though Wolf doesn't really like red roses, she chose the Wenlock rose from David Austin because it has a purplish hue, is very pro-lific, and has long arching canes.

opposite: In early spring at the back of the house near the pool, the nectarine tree is in bloom with tulips in the foreground. Later in the season Wolfe replaces the 1,500 tulips with dahlias. *ABOVE LEFT:* Wolfe discovered the fountain on the property and put it back in working order. The David Austin rose is called Golden Celebration. *ABOVE RIGHT:* The Farm section is where she keeps roses for cutting and experimenting with before planting. In the foreground is the fragrant sweet pea Painted Lady.

ABOVE LEFT: "I want fragrance, especially in roses," Wolf says. "If they don't deliver, they go." Full Sail is one of the only scented iceberg roses. *ABOVE RIGHT:* At the entrance to the secret garden are hydrangeas, Hero roses from David Austin, and fuschia arborescens. *OPPOSITE:* White cosmos grows in the foreground, with indigo spiraea and salvia climbing through the roses.

[*EXOTIC*]

Gardens are in Ana Roth's blood. Her grandparents, William and Lurline Roth, owned Filoli, the magnificent estate south of San Francisco, from 1937 until 1975, when Mrs. Roth donated the house and gardens to the National Trust for Historic Preservation. Ana Roth's maternal grandmother had a beautiful garden in Stockbridge, Massachussetts, and her mother has tended a garden in Ireland since 1964.

She only meant to stay in Los Angeles for a couple of years en route from New York to San Francisco. Eight years later she is still here, in a Hollywood Hills house that she selected with the help of the late Tony Duquette (see p. 194). Roth knew Duquette from childhood, and he was a huge influence in her life. "Tony got the design going—he put in the African panels that started the African room. And he taught me about layering plants," Roth says.

After thirteen years as a fashion stylist in New York, Roth gave an arms-wide-open welcome to the Mediterranean-style house with its overgrown tropical wilderness and Mexican tile pool. She bought the house precisely because of the potential that the gardens and the pool offered. "It was sad—someone had really loved the garden and put a lot of effort into it," she says. But it had been left untended and was an overgrown jungle. "*Sunset Boulevard* revisited," in the words of her friend, interior designer Nicky Nichols, who has been helping her pull the house and garden together.

At first, Roth fought to get the garden under control. A parade of landscape designers recommended that she tame it by cutting back and chopping down, and for a long time she fretted about what to do. "As soon as I gave in and let the garden be, I felt much happier," Roth says. "I just point it in the right direction now. Like a child, it has a will of its own."

For someone who loves to entertain, the Hollywood Hills house of Ana Roth provides a wealth of reclining possibilities. A soft alcove off the living room is for morning coffee and reading the paper. "I'm slowly taking different areas and bringing them back," she says.

Amid towering bamboo, banana, avocado and aloes, ash trees, and the bougainvillea that flows over the pergola are giant Italian pots, African tables and Indian mirrors. On a flat lot above is a lawn, her son's African playhouse, feathery acacia tree, grapefruit and lemon trees, roses, Mexican sage, vines, and orchids. The upper lot is her cutting garden and "the only area where I can weed and be hands-on," she says. Thanks to Nicky Nichols, an Asian influence is creeping in—Chinese pickle jars and Fu dog pots near elephant planters from Tony Duquette's buying trips to India—as are rare specimen plants like a black taro. About a year ago, they had the house checked for its feng shui. Out went a fountain with plants (bad water position); in came a coral front door (for warmth).

The 1927 house is a warren of rooms on many levels. Roth calls it a hamster cage that is ideal for parties not children, but her 11-year-old son loves it, and it has the flow that makes for a perfect party house. When Roth entertains, and she does frequently, she does so with great flair and in homage to a master. Tony Duquette arranged all of her grandmother's balls, and Roth remembers distinctly the impression made by hundreds of lanterns hanging in the oak trees. "Tony's parties spoiled me for life," she says. "He transformed a space and made everyone look beautiful and feel sexy. I aspire to that." For one party she brought out her collection of antique Kuba cloths, in homage to the time she spent living in Africa. For another, she hung five hundred Japanese lanterns around the pool and set out Pucci fabric-covered pillows in aqua, lime, and white.

"In New York it was all about dressing; that was my creative outlet. Here it's all about the house," Roth muses. "I love gardening. It's very meditative. Just half an hour after a bad day puts you in a better place."

TOP RIGHT: African benches and Italian pots line the brick-walled pool. "I didn't appreciate African art until I lived there," Roth says. *OPPOSITE AND RIGHT:* When she first moved into the house, she was overwhelmed by the masses of bougainvillea and the jungle feel of the timber bamboo. Now she embraces them.

Tony Duquette, an old family friend and a huge influence over Roth's taste, helped her choose the house and then got the interiors and gardens going. *LEFT:* Outside the living room are the African doors he brought in. *OPPOSITE:* "I like to blur the lines—mix antiques with modern," says Roth, who organizes her parties around themes. From her African collection come antique kuba cloths and tablecloths, chair covers, and baskets.

ABOVE: The bougainvillea-shaded arbor is an exotic blend of African textiles, baskets, and mirrors. Spring and summer are heavy with the scent of orange blossom, night-blooming jasmine, lilies, and plumeria (her grandmother had a house in Hawaii). *OPPOSITE:* Roth's son gets an African playhouse on an upper level of the garden.

As the film director responsible for such high-octane movies as *Independence Day* and *Godzilla*, Roland Emmerich has an eye for the large-scale and the dramatic, and that's exactly how his Los Angeles garden presents itself: it's bold and exuberant yet mysterious and hidden at the same time.

The mansion was built in 1918 for film producer Jesse Lasky (*The Squaw Man*, *The Great Caruso*) in what was then a fashionable part of Hollywood. Emmerich, who has lived in Los Angeles for about ten years, bought a romantic, neglected mess of a house that over the years had been sold to Mark Twain's daughter and then had been subjected to partitioning and subdividing by a series of renters. But he wanted privacy, and the house sat above the city on five acres, with some two acres of garden; it also abuts a state park.

Emmerich brought in architect Elizabeth Stevenson, who had just completed his home in Puerto Vallarta, and landscape designer Susan McEowen. He asked Stevenson for a house that evoked a crazy starlet from the 1920s—something mysterious, quirky, and from a different time. "My goal was to transform the house without obliterating what was there," she says. He wanted McEowen to make the garden lush with unusual plants that would complement the architecture and block out the roofline of the apartments below. "I'm not crazy about the view; it's not that great, except from the upstairs master bathroom," he explains.

Emmerich also requested that the grounds be reshaped to form an axis from the house down to the pool and poolhouse, based on the grand estates in Montecito he admires. "I wanted everything—the stairs, fountain, and the pool—to line up," he says. "But I didn't want it to be too ornate or Italian. It needed a very defined California feel." Adds

Like the set of a Cecil B. DeMille epic, the garden of director Roland Emmerich explodes with oversize banana trees and palms that match the grandeur of the 1918 Mediterranean estate. "I'm from Germany," Emmerich says. "To me, palm trees are exotic."

Stevenson, "The axis gives organization to something that otherwise would be chaotic." The symmetry of the stairs was offset by the asymmetrical house, which mixes Moroccan, Italian, and Spanish elements. While Stevenson added terraces to the dining and living rooms and removed the horseshoe driveway, McEowen was regrading the expansive front slope and reconfiguring the large trees—date, guava, palms, and butia, and giant bird of paradise.

As the design evolved, the garden became a blend of formal and informal, symmetry and asymmetry. Emmerich would go along on shopping expeditions for furniture, antiques, and plants and pots. Indian and Indonesian daybeds, columns and doors, Buddhas and statuary, and other antiques are scattered around the grounds. "If he likes something, he knows it immediately," say Stevenson. "He has a very strong focus." The terraces are filled with about four hundred pots. He wanted things lush and he wanted a lot of different plants, especially palms. "I'm German, so to me palm trees are exotic," he says. He loves strong colors, so the house is shades of turquoise, red, and yellow. The same bold mix happens in the garden—chartreuse leaves next to a deeper green with a shot of red.

The team was given free rein to buy the largest trees and plants they could find. "It was wonderful to work with mature, unusual plants," says Stevenson. "They give the garden a different dimension." Ponytail palms, double-trunk *pinus alapansus*, elephant's foot, cypresses, and *Washingtonia robusta* form a progression of tree heights. Clarke Cowan, who did the softscape and irrigation, brought in huge cactuses from his family's nursery in Malibu. Quirky and interesting succulents were ordered by mail from a nursery in Ohio.

Every inch of the garden was planned ahead of time and fine-tuned in the field. In the end, about five hundred different varieties of plants were used. The iceberg roses and sinuous expanse of lawn at the gates give a sense of sweeping space—there is no hint of the exotic garden that awaits above. "We're not giving everything away at once," says McEowen. "Unless you get inside, you have no idea what's there." Soon the house will be covered with vines, the canna lilies will be ten feet tall, and everything will be emphatically bigger and lusher. "I'm very impatient," says Emmerich, whose house and garden are the balance to his hectic life. "I keep telling the plants to grow."

"This wasn't about using the most expensive materials," Stevenson says. "It was about using evocative and unusual materials that were interesting and that wouldn't look like everyone else's backyard."

Emmerich, she adds, "has a vision, a romantic notion of old Hollywood. For the same amount of money he could have bought a home in Pacific Palisades. Here the area isn't that fashionable, but it gave him the land."

OPPOSITE: Architect Elizabeth Stevenson and landscape designer Susan McEowen brought in large, mature trees and fast-growing plants that will pump up the lushness and conceal the view. "Korean grass wraps around an aloe tree; albizia will cover the entrance stairwell," says McEowen.

ABOVE: Stevenson created straight axes around the house and grounds to give "organization to something that otherwise would be chaotic." *OPPOSITE:* David Austin roses are twined around palm trees in the entrance courtyard.

THIS PAGE: Emmerich, who has amassed a large collection of art and antiques through his travels, placed statues of Buddha, Indonesian chairs, and Indian benches around the grounds. *OVERLEAF:* A straight procession of stairs from the front door leads past a fountain down to the pool and poolhouse. "I wanted everything to line up, but I didn't want it to be too ornate or Italian. It needed a very defined California feel," he says.

To Garett Carlson, the site is everything. The landscape designer firmly believes that his clients should consult him first on any construction project—even before the architect—because he has an intuitive grasp of where all the structures should be placed on the land and how the garden should fit into the grand scheme. That attitude has won him some enemies among architects, but it has also brought him a loyal group of clients who have seen his philosophy at work.

For the Latana house in Point Dume, Malibu, altering the physical location of the beachfront structures was impossible. The house, a replica of a traditional Japanese residence, was built at the bottom of a cliff in the late 1960s for Rosemary and Hulsey Lokey (he was chairman of Host International). Everything was imported from Japan, including its distinctive roof made of thirteen thousand blue ceramic tiles, as well as an exact replica of the Torii shrine in the Inland Sea of Japan that sits on a bluff above the house and was blessed by Shinto monks.

But Carlson could sculpt the entire topside of this estate on a cliff and knock the land, which had essentially become a neglected mass of scorched, dry grass, back into shape. Since the entrance to the house is at the top, the garden is where he would have the most visual impact and influence.

His clients, Latana, a photographer and sculptor, and her husband, spent a long time selecting a landscape architect, but Latana says that as soon as she saw Carlson's black-and-white portfolio, she knew she had found the right person. "I'm a fine-art photographer," she says. "I responded to its Zen beauty."

As she is half-Asian, she and Carlson tapped into her heritage and that of the house to make the grounds relate to the architecture. "I appre-

LEFT: Perched on the edge of bluffs in Malibu, the Latana garden enjoys a sweeping view of the Santa Monica Bay, from Point Dume to Palos Verdes. It was Garett Carlson's job to grade the site to allow the view to dominate and bring in low-maintenance plants that could withstand the wind and ocean air.

77

ciated the quality and the spirit of the house," says Latana, who is bringing it back from a bachelor pad to its former glory. Carlson took the Japanese concept of "borrowed scenery"—linking elements to the background and making them look like they've always been there. And since Latana and her husband spend part of the year in Europe, having a low-maintenance garden was crucial.

Grading the site was key. "Grading is cheap and it gets more out of the space," says Carlson. He lowered the grade at the entrance specifically so that when the copper gates swing open, the impact of the ocean view is immediate. A dry creek bed was excavated and the dirt used to create soft, rounded mounds. Giant boulders were brought in by the truckload and placed in the creek bed like pieces of sculpture. He added Japanese pines, sycamores and fast-growers like mondo grass. "In a couple of years, the garden looked twenty-five years old; it was an immediate effect," Carlson says.

Latana studied books on Japanese gardens and she requested deciduous trees, whose leaves would die in winter and come back in the spring. "The sense of winter with leaves falling and the changing of seasons is nice for the garden," she says. An abundance of fruit trees—apples, lemons, figs, tangerine, peaches, cherries, lime, clementines, and avocado—flourish surprisingly well on the cliff edge. A line of pine trees; fruit trees; an arbor covered with wisteria and grapes; and lavender, jasmine, and irises were planted to camouflage the tennis court and caretaker's cottage.

As the driveway passes over the creek, the wood bridge creaks thanks to some planks that Carlson deliberately left loose. "Anything that stimulates the senses—how can you not love it," says Latana. Then begins the sharp descent, past the torii gate, down through an allée of bamboo to the house and studio that are on the beach. "I like the idea of discovery—everything here has to be big scale," she says.

Carlson excavated a dry creek bed and brought in giant boulders that were positioned around the property like sculptures. The 2 ½-acre property was ringed with sycamore, eucalyptus, and pine trees, and the lawn was seeded with fast-growing mondo grass.

ABOVE: An abundance of fruit trees flourish surprisingly well at the cliff's edge. *OPPOSITE:* The former owners had erected a replica of the Torii shrine in Japan's Inland Sea and had it blessed by Shinto monks. The house sits at the base of the bluffs and is connected to the garden by a series of walkways; its roof consists of 13,000 blue ceramic tiles imported from Japan.

[COUNTRY]

Judy Horton hasn't moved far from where she was raised. Her parents moved to Hancock Park in 1959, and this neighborhood in Los Angeles is where she went to high school, where she married and lived, and, after her divorce, bought her own house in 1983.

Her house hasn't moved far either. It was built in the 1920s for the Janns family, who developed Westwood, and was moved to its current location in 1945. The Janns' son lived on one side and the mother on the other, with the garden in between. Horton immediately redid the front and center walkway; then she started to contemplate the back. All she had to work with were a pergola, an old tree trunk supporting the climbing roses, and a boxwood path.

Horton has always been a gardener—she started when she was a little girl—and in the early 1980s she began to consider a career change. "There's something about a woman in her forties—an urge to get into the garden and get your hands into the dirt," she says, echoing a common refrain. She took University of California Los Angeles's landscape architecture program, did a gazillion sketches, and was paralyzed with too many ideas. She dropped out of the program and hired one of her classmates, Frances Knight, and the two began collaborating on Horton's garden. "We spent a year sketching on paper," Horton recalls. Both read Gertrude Jekyll's writings; both were in love with English garden rooms. They worked all the way through 1989 and installed it in 1990. They put in roses, herbs, and Mediterranean plants. "The only thing we didn't put in was bamboo," Horton says.

Horton couldn't absorb plant knowledge fast enough. She traveled, went to lectures, took advanced courses, and became an avid reader. Friends started asking for help with their gardens. She formed a partnership with

English country with a California twist—punches of orange, red and purple—is how the garden of landscape designer Judy Horton has evolved. The bower of the Craftsman house supports the white roses that give her fragrance in the living room and upstairs office.

Cheryl Lerner in 1993. They worked together until 1997, when Judy M. Horton Garden Design opened for business.

Her own garden is English country—the fence and box hedges form its basic structure, and she knew she wanted to grow perennials and bulbs. But she has given it a distinct California twist. "The English talk about unifying a garden with gray," Horton says. "I used purples, orange, and reddish browns. I love the color orange in southern California. My other passion is fruit trees. Persimmon . . . pomegranates—they have become my trademark. The one that inspired me was in my uncle's garden in Colorado. Stone fruit don't work, but apples are very happy here."

She turned the back garage into a potting shed and the hot back section is where she puts dry Mediterranean plants—lavender, rosemary, bay, ceanothus—and where she lets things take over and seed. "I change the area around at will. I grew corn but now it's grasses; I'm going back to my midwestern roots, back to the Nebraska prairie." She always tells her clients to conjure up images from childhood or their travels. "You should feel transported in a garden," she says. "My feeling is that a garden needs to match the personality of the owner, the architecture, and the neighborhood, in that order."

The front of the house, in contrast, is dark and shady. She wanted to create a view from her front picture windows with foliage not flowers, so she went deciduous—a Rangpor lime (a decorative citrus used in the 1920s and 1930s), coral bark maple, and a Chinese elm that traps moisture and gives filtered shade.

Horton has a demanding garden. "It needs a great deal of attention. I'm usually in the garden an hour a day looking, thinking, snipping," she says. "There is no downtime for gardens in Southern California. Summer is the time to cut way back. I think of August as our winter. But I don't want a garden in which I don't have anything to do."

Horton's garden goes through subtle shifts. "Originally I was drawn to texture and seasonal change—I like a plant to show me different things," she says. "But I'm coming around to wanting uniformity. Plants never stay still. Things don't always go as planned. I'm not always in control, just the guiding hand."

"English garden rooms are successful with avid plantspeople," says Horton, who applies Gertrude Jekyll's lessons, but on a reduced scale. "When Jekyll talks about her color theories, she's talking one hundred yards, not thirty feet." The rooms around the grape bower are planted with lightly fragrant things: a tree gardenia ("in 1983 it was a little plant"), a compact variety of magnolia with a lemony scent, lilies, nicotiana, a sweet olive, and a weeping white wisteria at nose level.

ABOVE: Horton wanted the view from the front windows to be of foliage, not flowers, so all is deciduous and shade—a Chinese elm, coral bark maple, Rangpor lime. *OPPOSITE:* At the back of the garden is her potting shed and hot section, where she constantly changes plants around. She grows tomatoes, basil, arugula, figs, and wild strawberries. A weeping mulberry that loses leaves in winter becomes "very sculptural." Taking her cue from landscaper Andrew Kao, she tops pots with glass pebbles—"glass is great for mulching succulents."

The pedigree was impeccable. The three-story house on a steep hillside in Silver Lake was designed in the 1950s by renowned modernist architect Rudolf Schindler. But while the gray house was carefully sited to take in the view of the lake, the garden seemed an afterthought. The rear hillside, which drops down to the street below, was a haphazard series of rubble and cinderblock terraces that were covered with weeds and bore no relation to the house.

"If you squinted, the weeds looked like a meadow," says landscape designer Judy Kameon, charitably. She was asked by her clients Connie Butler, a curator at the Museum of Contemporary Art (MoCA) in Los Angeles, and David Schafer, an artist and teacher, to bring the grounds into harmony with the house. Kameon has an affinity for modern architecture—her father is an architect—and she has gained a reputation over the past six years for her landscape work on classic mid-century modern residences by Schindler, Richard Neutra, Gregory Ain, and A. Quincy Jones, as well as contemporary houses.

For Kameon, the architecture always comes first. Her training as a painter at University of California Los Angeles gave her the tools for working with perspective, scale, and color. Her career change occurred when she bought her own house and an adjacent empty lot and became obsessed with gardening. She opened a restaurant in the middle of her garden, and among her guests was club impresario and restaurateur Sean McPherson. She designed a garden for him; commissions from Spike Jonze, Sofia Coppola, and other hip Hollywood denizens followed. Now her company, Elysian Landscapes, is a full-fledged design firm

"Some clients want minimal graphic plantings to stay in line with their modern house, some want to play against it. With this house, I think we did both," says Judy Kameon. The Rudolf Schindler house sits above a steep slope in Silver Lake. "It is an elegant and imposing edifice when you are below, looking up," says the landscape designer. "It's also framed by huge and beautiful old eucalyptus trees on either side, which give a sense of scale."

ABOVE LEFT: Kameon added a terrace, bench-stairs, and built-in planters to link the house with the garden. "They are clean simple structures and are very much in keeping with the house. I wanted it to feel like a natural extension of the house, which has built-in seating and planters." *ABOVE RIGHT:* Because of the steep drop, Kameon created a "strolling garden" with a path that zigzags through the plants. *OPPOSITE:* She enhanced the meadow effect with tall grasses.

and she is producing a line of outdoor furniture called Plain Air with partner Eric Ostea.

The first decision at the Schindler house was to build a broad terrace directly outside the living room that is covered with decomposed granite. The steps double as seats and built-in planters, which was done to duplicate Schindler's built-in furnishings and planters inside and thus bring him into the garden. "The terraces, bench/stairs, and planters are clean, simple structures and are very much in keeping with the house; they are a natural extension of it," Kameon says. "The house is so strong, but there was no consideration for the use of the outdoor space."

The terrace also serves as an important transition from the strong house to the soft garden. Next came a stairway that zigzags past ground cover of rosemary, gazanias, fruit trees, Mexican sage, junipers, and salvia. Since the site is so steep, Kameon turned it into a strolling garden. She preserved the meadow effect of the weeds with plantings of grasses of all shapes and sizes. Everything was meant to be low-maintenance and to prevent soil erosion. The stairway also gave the garden a logical structure that had been missing before. The fruit trees ended up in one quadrant and were defined with landscape ties that made them visually cohesive and allowed Butler and Schafer to pick the fruit. Since the garden is primarily experienced from the upper terrace, windows, and balconies, Kameon used large-scale plants that would read from above and planted them in a very graphic way. Color was an added layer. When they did the installation, Kameon had one member of her crew stationed at the top and one at the bottom of the garden with walkie-talkies, shouting instructions, while she climbed up and down positioning the plants.

"When you are below, looking up, the house is an imposing, elegant edifice," Kameon says. "It is framed by huge, beautiful eucalyptus trees on either side, which also give a sense of its scale. The garden has a different character. It has a lot of color, texture, and movement and is more geared to human scale."

"The garden has a very different character than the house," says Kameon. "It has a lot of color and texture and movement and is more geared to human scale."

"I was born in 1934. I remember Sunset Boulevard when it was bridle path," says Barbara Howard, who provides one of the strongest links to the Hollywood of another age. Her father Jack Warner ruled Hollywood in Warner Bros.' heyday, and he and his wife Ann entertained regally from a grand estate at the top of Beverly Hills (now owned by David Geffen). The house was decorated by William Haines, one of the top Los Angeles designers in the 1950s and 1960s. The gardens were created by Florence Yoch, one of the most influential landscape designers of the period.

Since 1975 Howard has lived above now-busy Sunset Boulevard in Holmby Hills, an enclave tucked between Westwood, Bel-Air, and Beverly Hills. The house was built in 1953 by her late husband Cy Howard, television writer and director of *My Friend Irma* and producer of numerous Jerry Lewis movies. In the opening scenes of the 1955 Jack Palance movie *Big Knife*, the narrator sets up the tale of a small-town boxer who makes it big; shots of swank Beverly Hills mansions are shown, including the Howard house, looking much as it does today.

"Cy heard the land was for sale, so he drove up here. George McLean was there; he was sitting under an olive tree, drawing a spec house," Barbara Howard relates. McLean was a talented local builder who never trained as an architect but who was doing houses around town for various stars—Elizabeth Taylor and Robert Stack were early clients. He and Cy Howard hit it off and they began building a cross between a Danish hunting lodge and a Cliff May ranch house. "Unfortunately, by the time they got to the back, Cy had run out of money, so it's a warren of tiny rooms and a garage," says Howard, who is slowly renovating the house.

But the scale of the ranch house is perfectly suited to its three-acre site. A steep driveway curves up and away from Sunset and the cars. The

Within the three-acre woodland of Barbara Howard's house is a path that leads to her secret garden. She and landscape designer Barry Sattels found a pair of nineteenth-century iron elevator doors and brick columns and built the entrance to her "dark and beautiful spot."

gravel drive sweeps past an old-fashioned but fully automatic split-rail gate and meanders around to the house at the top of the knoll. Two years ago a landslide washed away most of the gravel driveway, and it forced Barbara Howard to finally put in a retaining wall. "I kept hearing Cy's voice saying, 'Don't build it.' I would reply, 'You can't possibly see everything.'" She did keep the old wood gate and gravel. "Cy would have wanted it kept that way, but I can't tell you how much it's taken to maintain."

She asked landscape designer Barry Sattels to help shape the grounds. "Barbara is elegant and wonderfully simple," Sattels says, "and the garden reflects her personality." Sattels saw his mission as simply enhancing the natural woodland. "I preserved the old forest and took out the junk. I culled deadwood but left it as wild as possible, just interlacing trees for support. It was great because there was an immediate result," he says.

The garden was covered with old olive and lemon trees. Sattels brought in Mediterranean plantings, lavender, morning glories, and succulents, as well as hydrangeas, agapanthus, grasses, ivy, and 2,000 daffodils, jonquils, and tulip bulbs.

They found a pair of brick columns and nineteenth-century elevator gates and constructed a doorway that leads from the main garden into "a secret garden, a dark and beautiful spot," says Sattels. In the secret garden is a table and chairs where Howard and friends eat on summer evenings; the path continues on to a treehouse, complete with lights and electricity, that Howard constructed for her grandchildren. "I've always wanted to build something from scratch," she says. "It was the most fun thing I've done in years." An old doghouse that belonged to her parents' Irish wolfhound became her granddaughter's playhouse.

There are a few mementos of Hollywood scattered around the house and grounds. Few Jacuzzis in town have as interesting a background: Howard's sculpted spa was created in 1977 by Maj Hagman, the wife of actor Larry Hagman, in the pre-*Dallas* days.

Howard loves houses and gardens. She has homes in Palm Springs, New York, and Paris. She loves roses, and she loves to cook, so she grows basil, mint, parsley, and tomatoes. But she admits she is not much of a gardener, so the low-maintenance woodland in Holmby Hills suits her perfectly. "I travel a lot and I can't stay on top of a garden," she says. "My pied-à-terre in Paris has about five flower pots, and that's perfectly manageable."

OPPOSITE TOP LEFT AND RIGHT: The path heads down to an entertaining area and then to a playhouse, complete with electricity, that Howard designed for her grandchildren. "I've always wanted to build something from scratch," she says. "It was the most fun thing I've done in years." *BOTTOM RIGHT:* The ranch house built by her late husband Cy Howard is pretty much the same as when it was built in 1953. *BOTTOM LEFT:* Above Sunset Boulevard, yet a world away, the grounds are a mix of old woodland and olive trees with Mediterranean plantings brought in by Sattels.

[FORMAL]

There aren't many producers/talent managers who admit to spending their Sundays gardening. But for Keith Addis, gardening is therapy. "I love deadheading and planting," he says. "It gets my mind out of work. I do all the repotting and pick out all the plants."

The Hollywood house that he and his wife, Keri Selig, have lived in for three years was built in 1922. It sits high in the hills, and from the gardens and the upper balconies the city unfolds in a very immediate way. The Hollywood freeway roars past in the distance—a constant stream of cars moving in two directions. "We love the sound of the freeway—it's like a river," says Keri. "At night, it's a magnificent site. It's like a living neon sign. And the ribbon of traffic never ceases."

The Addises are the fifth owners, and although the house has had some illustrious occupants, including historians Will and Ariel Durant, it was not in the best condition when they arrived. But it was an unusual combination: Spanish Colonial revival with Craftsman influences. There is a round entrance tower, dark wood beams and paneling, beautifully proportioned rooms, and a grand curving staircase in the front hall. The Addises, working with contractor Sam Schatz and interior designer Jenny Armit, brought the house back to its Hollywood roots. "The challenge was to make the house comfortable on a contemporary level without disturbing the architecture," Keith says. "The whole concept was based on my idealized vision of Veronica Lake," he adds. "If she had had money and taste in the 1940s, what would she have done?" In homage to Lake, a black-and-white portrait of the pouty star hangs in an upstairs hallway.

The distinctive lawn and clipped hedges were in terrible shape and the fountain in the circular front courtyard hadn't worked in twenty years.

Tightly clipped box hedges and immaculate lawns are precisely how Keith Addis and Keri Selig like their English garden kept. Addis, who is a top talent manager and producer, says that doing the gardening on weekends is his form of therapy.

The house belonged at one time to historians Will and Ariel Durant. By the time the Addises bought it, it was overgrown and rundown, but the bones were still there. They spent ten months bringing it back to life. *OVERLEAF:* The fountain in the front motorcourt hadn't worked in twenty years. Addis installed 600 sprinkler heads. Using the Japanese elms and mature palm trees as a backdrop, he filled in with banks of roses and lilies.

"But the bones of the garden—the English box hedges—were totally there," Keith says. They redid the entry courtyard, putting in masses of pink roses. They added an entire back deck, redid the tennis court, and installed six hundred sprinkler heads to water the immaculately kept lawns and box hedges. "It takes two guys, twice a week for eight hours to water—thirty-two hours a week of maintenance," he notes. Japanese elms that frame the perimeter of the two-acre property and twenty-five mature palm trees and cypresses were already in place. The Addises planted fruit trees—oranges, figs, pomegranate, avocado, satsumas and elephant plums. Outside the perimeter wall are juvenile plantings of cactus and aloe—Keith's first foray into the succulent world. They renovated the back patio. Outside the kitchen they added a porch with a wood-burning fireplace. The entire project—house and garden—took ten months. "That's why he's such a good producer," notes Keri wryly, who is a successful film producer in her own right. Forays to the Rose Bowl flea market and other swap meets yielded a cache of 1930s and 1940s Bauer pots. "My obsession is the indoor flowers, his is the outdoor," says Keri, who keeps eighteen vases in the house filled with freshly cut flowers from the garden.

In his autobiography *Another Life* (Random House, 1999), editor Michael Korda offered a glimpse into the house when he recounts a rare visit to Will and Ariel Durant, the historians and writers who lived there:

"Whatever had brought them to the West Coast from New York in the first place, they lived in resentful seclusion among the ravines and steep, wooded hills of North Hollywood, unfindable without elaborate directions and a map. Back in the day of silent pictures, this had been a fashionable neighborhood, though its aspect was sinister and strangely dark for L.A.: winding, narrow roads, high walls with dense shrubbery concealing grotesque houses and huge overhanging trees, all combined to produce an atmostphere that was more Transylvanian than Californian....Their home, what could be seen of it behind stone walls and fiercely overgrown vegetation, was in the 1920s Hollywood Spanish Gothic style, with much wrought iron, heavy wooden doors, gargoyles, tiny barred windows, and carved oak shutters..."

These days, the house and grounds are more user-friendly. Keith and Keri were married in their garden a year ago. "There were tons of flowers floating in the pool," Keri says. "The chupah was made of bougainvillea that we planted on the property."

Suzanne Rheinstein's garden is formal and proper—perfectly in keeping with her New Orleans roots and the architecture of the neo-Georgian/Colonial house in Windsor Square, where she and her husband Fred have lived for twenty-two years.

"I didn't want to buy the house; I was into gardening and there was a big pool surrounded by cement and red brick," she says. "But Fred adored it, so we agreed on a garden budget and I spent it all on the front." It took her seventeen years to move the pool.

Rheinstein is the owner of Hollyhock, a West Hollywood store filled with a unique mix of antique furniture, fabrics, accessories, and books. Her design firm, Suzanne Rheinstein & Associates, is responsible for an assortment of elegant interiors around the country. She has absorbed design and garden lessons from her travels and from a host of teachers. She worked with James Yoch (grandnephew of the great landscape designer Florence Yoch) on the front garden and with Judy Horton (see p. 84) on the back. "Judy totally supported me in my quest for an organic garden," she says. Through Ruth Morley, she became involved with the Huntington Gardens. "Ruth opened my eyes; she was passionate about roses," says Rheinstein. "That's how I got the Lady Banks roses—the glory of spring. I worked as a volunteer at the Huntington's plant sales with a small group of incredibly knowledgeable gardeners."

The Rheinsteins are the third family to live in the house since 1913, and Suzanne felt that the house deserved a garden with structure and geometry. "All the years we've lived here I've drawn and redrawn the backyard," she says. "Fred wanted a crisp garden; I didn't want a fluffy garden and I didn't want to re-create an English garden." With Horton, she created axes and a sense of progression by finally moving the pool

Working with garden designer Judy Horton, Suzanne Rheinstein slowly brought her garden into line. She moved the pool from the center to the rear and put in a circular pond and created a quiet zone of green and grays. "It's a quiet garden," she says. "You are richly rewarded when you notice the details."

back where a paddle tennis court stood idle. Green and gray shapes and gravel dominate the area around the house. "It's a quiet garden," she notes. "You are richly rewarded when you notice the details." A woodland garden transitions into a gravel garden, a cutting garden, and then, past a fence of quince and three types of fig trees, the salad garden. That is where tarragon, heirloom tomatoes, fennel, artichokes, and succulents grow large and a red passionflower overflows a French bower. It's where, Rheinstein says, "I can be as messy as I want."

They recently added a porch. "It's very tropical, very New Orleans," Rheinstein says. "It provides shelter from the sun. Loggia living is part of a gracious way of life—it offers a pleasant place to eat and read the paper, and enjoy the garden." They took the old garage—the former owners had their own gas pump and the chauffeur's quarters were upstairs—and turned it into a poolhouse where they entertain. "The pool area is our vulgar hot garden with pots of citrus, kumquats, satsumas, fraises de bois," she says. "If you live in California, you have to have citrus trees, herbs, and pots."

In the beginning, she thought that flowers and color were important. "I've always loved simple flowers like a single white rose. I have a hard time loving hybrid tea roses—they are unattractive, big, blowsy, and loud." Now she prefers strong colors, shapes, and texture. "I'm mad about coleus and tropicals. I love the romance of big things in front of smaller things. I love green architecture. In the South, it gets too hot for flowers." The garden is also about memories and scent: A climbing rose outside her daughter's upstairs bedroom; concentric pots buried in the soil, an idea she took from Gertrude Jekyll; datura. "About twelve years ago I saw Nancy Lancaster's garden and she grew brugmansia," Rheinstein recalls. "In the evening, it's a heavenly scent."

Rheinstein is now content to appreciate the small changes in her garden. For her, one of life's greatest pleasures is hand-watering in the late afternoon. "I like to open myself to new things," Suzanne Rheinstein says. "Perfection isn't good for us."

TOP AND BOTTOM RIGHT: In the front, Lady Banks roses are a graceful counterpart to the neo-Georgian architecture of columns and brickwork. *OPPOSITE:* A new porch relates to her New Orleans roots. "Loggia living is part of a gracious way of life," Rheinstein says. "The porch offers a pleasant place to eat, read the paper, and enjoy the garden." Plants like the elephant's ear speak to her love of contrast—dark purply brown and chartreuse, black and chartreuse.

At the back, where a paddle tennis court once stood, is now the pool and her "vulgar hot garden." "If you live in California, you have to have citrus trees, herbs, and pots," says Rheinstein, who furnished the area with pieces from her West Hollywood store Hollyhock.

Rheinstein is an avid traveler and a reader of garden literature. Some of her inspiration came from trips "with a group of garden fanatics" to Provence, in particular to La Louve, the garden of designer Nicole de Vésian, and some from trips to the Cotswolds. *ABOVE LEFT AND RIGHT:* "The garden is not too floriforous," she says. "There are lots of things with berries—Virginia creeper, red oak, myrtle, pyracantha." *OPPOSITE:* Outside the poolhouse, the clipped gravel garden transitions to a wilder, more flamboyant section. *OVERLEAF:* "Here I can be as messy as I want," she says. A red passionflower overflows a bower. Fruit trees (three types of figs, apples, guava, loquats, persimmon), Burmese honeysuckle, and single and double old-fashioned roses abound.

[*TROPICAL*]

From the front, Marilyn Wilson and Scooter Pietsch's house looks like any other sprawling bungalow in California's San Fernando Valley—mature shade trees, lawn, single-story ranch house (in this case, a 1930s Spanish bungalow with old wood beams and tiled floors).

Step through the house and into the back garden, however, and you are transported into a tropical paradise—a fantasy resort filled with palm trees of all shapes and sizes, giant banana trees, and thirty-foot-tall clumping bamboo stands. "We like the surprise factor," says Marilyn. "You don't expect it."

Marilyn and Scooter have an aerial photograph of the house, taken in 1938, that shows scattered houses and some neighboring lots under water—the result of a flood that necessitated the photo and would lead to the construction of the Sepulveda Dam. There isn't one tree on the property. Their entire one hundred-by-three hundred-foot lot is naked, save for the house. Along the way, someone planted a magnolia, mulberry, giant sycamore, and pine tree; a swimming pool was added in 1954, but the garden lay fallow.

When Marilyn (a television producer, most recently of "Politically Incorrect") and Scooter (a music composer for TV and movies) came upon the house four years ago, they walked through it, saw the huge dirt backyard and said, "We'll take it." "It was a nice Spanish house and we saw the possibilities," says Marilyn.

They found landscape architect Garett Carlson through a friend, and he drew up the structural bones of the garden. Marilyn and Scooter were married eleven years ago on the north shore of Kauai, and they are drawn to the

For Marilyn and Scooter, the look they wanted for their garden was obvious—a tropical oasis that reminded them of Hawaii, where they were married. "We once rented a Spanish house that had an outdoor fireplace," says Scooter. "One evening we lit it and everyone gravitated to it and we wanted one ever since." The palapa draws their guests even in winter or when it's raining.

ABOVE LEFT: A Buddha head sits amid the palm and banana trees and the bamboo. "We like to walk the garden at least once a week to see what's going on, what's growing and taking over entire sections," says Marilyn. "And we've become better at knowing the cycle of the plants." *ABOVE RIGHT:* An expanse of lawn is for playing football and baseball and for their kids to run around and play on. "Our landscape designer Garett Carlson suggested this tunnel of grass, because it makes the garden look longer than it is," notes Scooter. *OPPOSITE:* Their son Riley enjoys the outdoor shower. Water pours from bamboo spouts, and shells from a beach in Hawaii are embedded in the cement.

greenery of the tropics. "Hawaii is so beautiful and lush—that's the feeling we wanted to capture," says Marilyn, who had spent a year clipping pages from magazines (mainly *Garden Design* and *Architectural Digest*) and books. "We had a scrapbook of pictures, mostly from Bali, Indonesia, and Hawaii, showing plants we liked. But we had no idea if anything would work in Southern California," she adds. So, like any super-efficient executive producer, she did her research. She looked through *10,000 Plants*, an encyclopedic reference book, in its entirety and wrote down every single plant that would work. Most retail nurseries had never heard of the plants, and they certainly didn't have them in stock. So together with Carlson and his landscape contractor, Brian Diamond, Marilyn and Scooter took a crash course in buying tropical wholesale.

"Garett drew up the basic bones and the flow," says Scooter, "but we wanted to be very involved in the plant picking. We were very hands-on. We really enjoyed the process, especially tree shopping. There are these huge dirt lots under the power lines that follow the grid from Orange County to Los Angeles County. No one wants to live under them, so the utility companies rent the land to nurseries. It's a surreal experience walking around them; some grow five hundred of just one kind of tree."

They bought king, queen, blue royal, and Washington palms; ginger; plumeria; pineapple guava; New Guinea impatiens; ferns; taro; canna lilies; kangaroo paw; and red hot pokers. Rosemary and lavender were planted liberally everywhere.

Then they spent two weeks living with their stash of three thousand potted plants and sixty-five trees before they started planting them in the ground, continually moving them around and shifting them until they got the sequence just right: the exact number of undulating beds, the views (and privacy) they wanted, and the right curve of queen palms that circle the thatched-roof palapa. "It's not like building a house where, once you've put the walls up, you're stuck," says Scooter. "You can't change a window. With a garden, you can visualize how much curve to give the beds."

Today the garden gives off a truly tropical vibe. The flowers are all in rich, saturated oranges, reds, and purples—bright colors to bounce off all the green. "It's a loose garden; it's not manicured," says Marilyn. "Friends come over and they really relax, like they're on vacation. And, just like a resort, they leave feeling refreshed."

The garden's personality matches Scooter's, says Marilyn. He is a very earthy, tactile person, and the garden reflects that—it is lush, with soft lines and voluptuous plants. The soil is very fertile—plants quickly grow tall and thick. Some have grown five feet in the past three years.

The garden has, in fact, become their escape, and they live their lives in it—eating, reading, swimming, hanging out. "It's peaceful and relaxing," says Marilyn. "Neither of us are sun worshippers—we just like being outside. I wanted to come home at the end of a stressful day and be able to stare out and not feel like I'm in the middle of Los Angeles."

The double bed under the mulberry tree is, says Marilyn, "our take on the Sky Bar at the Mondrian hotel." The couple entertains frequently outside. "Eating outside is a better dining experience than inside," says Marilyn. "You can be messier and more informal." The dining table is made of antique doors from Pakistan.

Scooter works from home in a new office/studio they built at the back. For the interiors, he wanted banks of windows so that he could work in natural light and look out onto the garden. "It's very conducive to creative thinking and a great place to have meetings," he says. And while he doesn't want lights on inside during the day, at night it's a different story. "I am so into lights—it makes the garden feel magical," he says. "Every tree and bush, even the back wall, has white Christmas lights."

Interspersed unobtrusively among the trees and plants are Buddha heads, Indonesian benches, Indian doors, and Balinese statues. The winding path leads past three key relaxation spots to which guests gravitate—a giant bed under the mulberry tree, the outdoor fireplace that's shaded by a thatched-roof palapa, and a covered bench at the far end of the garden. "At night, the bench has one of the best views through the trees all the way to the house," says Scooter.

The magic isn't only for adults. The Wilsons cleverly figured that if they created a really cool garden, their two kids would want to hang out in it, too. Their son Riley and a friend recently spent an entire afternoon camping out with tents, water, backpacks, and cameras, exploring different hidden nooks and crannies and taking photos.

Now that they have created the ultimate retreat, the Wilsons never want to leave. "We hate going out; we much prefer hanging out here," says Marilyn. "We love to have dinner parties and entertain and cook. We're not house users—we're outside all the time. Eating outside is a better dining experience than inside—you can be messier and more informal. We gave a party in February; even in winter thirty guests were gathered outside around the fireplace."

The garden has become an integral part of their lives. For their tenth anniversary, Marilyn planned a surprise party. She turned the basketball court into a Parisian café, with small round tables, and she hired all the musicians who had worked on a song Scooter wrote; he and fifty guests got to hear it played live for the first time. Their assistant presented them with another special gift—a book filled with snapshots of the garden that captured all its tiny intimate details, from vines creeping around statues to trees covered in lights. The Wilsons have lived in houses before, and they had tended small gardens, but this is their first real garden project and this is the first place they really call home. "I'm an army brat," says Marilyn. "I have no roots. I've spent all my life traveling around the world. This garden has given me a sense of stability."

"Landscaping can be very expensive," adds Scooter. "You can spend a fortune because you see another tree or plant that you just have to have. And sometimes you regret spending money on certain things. But I've never had any regret about the money we spent on the garden. It has made such an improvement in our lives."

The Spanish house dates to the 1930s. The Wilsons created a cabana and wet bar out of the old garage and had the side painted with a mural of their three favorite beaches in Hawaii. At the same time that the hardscape went in, the garden was completely wired for sound and light.

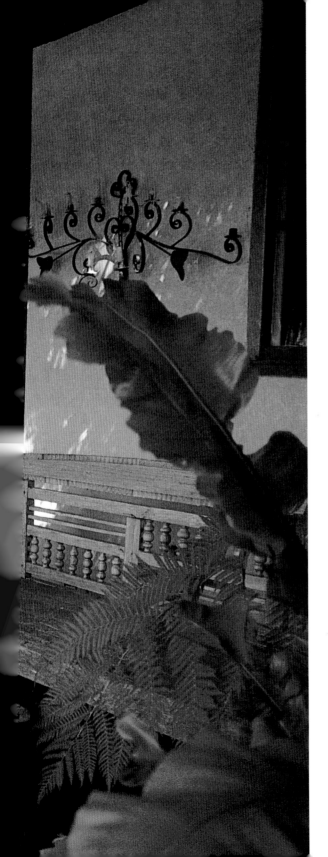

It took a massive landslide to give Lisa Bittan her garden.

Bittan had moved into her Santa Monica Canyon house in 1993 and lived there happily with her son, enjoying the garden even though there was no view of the canyon because giant pine and eucalyptus trees bordered the ravine's edge. Then one afternoon in 1998 she came home to a scene of total chaos—helicopters, sirens, and the street cordoned off. The entire back of her property had slipped down a hundred feet to the narrow street below. The towering trees were gone. Her backyard was destroyed. Her son's playhouse was teetering on the edge of the cliff. It took two years of major construction to sink in a new retaining wall. But she gained about five more feet of land and, of course, she gained a view.

Out of that chaos emerged a radically new garden. It went from being a shade garden to a tropical sun garden. Bittan consulted with landscape designer Curt Klebaum on the concept, but she says she kept changing her mind so often that she eventually took over the planting herself. "I kept changing the scale," she says. "I wanted bigger, lusher, more varied." Klebaum planted bird of paradise and phlox. Bittan added orange lantana, cannas, agaves, giant aloes, angel's trumpet, bougainvillea, and persimmon. Her main inspiration was Majorelle, the exuberantly exotic garden in Marrakesh that was planted in the 1920s by architect and painter Jacques Majorelle and is now owned by Yves Saint Laurent, and the succulent gardens she saw in Merida, Mexico. "I travel a lot. I like to go to exotic places and I spend a lot of time in the tropics," Bittan says. Wherever she goes—plantations in South Carolina, Mexico, the Caribbean, and China—she makes it a point to visit local gardens. Now the garden is all jungle and succulents, and everything—giant bird of paradise, lantana, and banana trees—was planted after 1998.

An old fig tree and a wisteria are tightly entwined around the trellis that shades Lisa Bittan's terrace. "The doors are open all the time, unless it's freezing," Bittan says. "Our whole life revolves around the terrace." Pots of jasmine and gardenias give pockets of fragrance year-round.

The house has its own interesting history. It was built by John M. Chapman, a Scotsman who lived in Los Angeles and made his living as an interior designer to stars such as Ronald Coleman and Cary Grant. Chapman lived next door and in the 1950s on his neighboring lot, built a Spanish Colonial concoction of leaded glass windows, antique columns and doorposts, old tile, and meandering rooms. Before Bittan moved in, Ned Tanen (a prominent Hollywood executive), Jeff Berg (head of ICM talent agency), and Joan Houseman (widow of actor John Houseman) had each added individual touches.

The house was built so that all the rooms overlook the garden. An ancient gnarled fig and wisteria are wrapped tightly around the trellis that shades the terrace. "Our whole life revolves around the terrace," Bittan says. "We have all our meals out here and the doors are open all the time, unless it's freezing." All the plants that were saved after the landslide—jasmine, gardenias, ferns, and sago palms—were put into pots and now stud the terrace.

The lawn plays its own specific role: "When the adults are sitting under the trellis, the lawn becomes an outdoor living theater where the kids play and roll down the hills," Bittan says.

ABOVE: Tall pine and eucalyptus trees had once shrouded the garden in shade. After the 1998 landslide, Bittan turned it into a sun garden, a combination of jungle and succulents with plants copied from the Majorelle garden in Morocco and the desert landscape in Merida, Mexico. *OPPOSITE:* Orange, red, yellow, and purple are the predominant shades. Everything—canna lilies, hibiscus, lantana, datura, aloes, agave, bird of paradise—was planted after 1998. Architectural details, such as leaded glass windows and antique columns, are interspersed around the property.

Susan Cohen's garden has come a long way from its Mexican tile pavers, avocado trees, crummy picket fence, and a single-car garage in back. Now it is an extension of her love of Orientalism—a small jewel box of bamboo, water, orchids and Buddhas—where scale is everything and every inch counts. It is a bit of Bali in Santa Monica.

On a trip to Bali two years ago, the interior designer was captivated by the way people live. "The outside was the inside; the outdoors is part of the indoor experience," she says. "I decided to create interior spaces outside."

But she needed help, and she found it in the shape of two kindred spirits. "I saw Thomas Schoos's garden store and fell in love with him and his raw talent," Cohen says. "I knew instantly that he was the one to collaborate with on the garden. He's a generous spirit and we are on the same wavelength creatively." Schoos has taken Los Angeles by storm with his landscaping practice and design stores that showcase his idiosyncratic mix of giant Buddha head fountains, water features, bamboo, and Indonesian garden antiques.

But first Cohen turned to pool maestro David Tisherman, who installed a lap pool. "David is another creative spirit, right up my alley, and again it was love at first sight," says Cohen. "I didn't want a normal pool. Mine is more of a water element. It has an infinity edge and the front and back are shallow ledges."

She put in a concrete wall around the property, which gave it more of a contemporary touch, and converted the garage into her design office. Then she was ready to plant. "As a designer, I look at the background space before I fill in the plans," says Cohen. Timber bamboo went in first—it gave the garden height and created privacy. In the last couple of

Inspired by a trip to Bali, Susan Cohen turned her Santa Monica garden into a Balinese fantasy. The interior designer worked with David Tisherman on the lap pool and spa, and with Thomas Schoos on the palapa, which is attached to the house and is covered with handwoven thatch from Indonesia.

years, it has grown tall enough to hide any unsightly telephone poles. She only planted things that she could cut and bring into the house—agapanthus (African lily), calla lilies, and orchids. "I wove the orchids into the trees and into the giant bird of paradise," Cohen says. "I'm always searching for something that no one else has, and most people have orchids in pots, not in trees." The ground cover is a tapestry of baby's tears, moss, and several kinds of mondo grass that looks like a piece of woven fabric. "There is some repetition and balance—I didn't want too many things," she adds. Like her interiors, precision is everything. "I'm afraid to order plants out of catalogs," she admits. "I have to see everything, touch everything. I'm so controlling I have to pick out the single perfect plant. And I'm bored easily, so I'm constantly moving things around. That's why all the plants are in pots."

Schoos designed the palapa around some nineteenth-century Indian columns. The roof was covered with handmade woven thatch from Indonesia and chair fabric hangs from each corner. Schoos also created a Buddha fountain and fish pond. "It adds one more layer, like design, which is a layering of styles, periods, and parts of the world that create a whole environment," says Cohen. "The garden is hundreds of years of design from around the world."

Once the water elements, flowers, and colors were in place, Cohen was ready to add the final sensual touches: music ("an important element for the Zen quality—the sound of music and water relate to each other") and scent ("I burn incense and candles that are very intoxicating").

Now on weekends she and her husband stay in the garden as much as possible. "We eat lunch and dinner there. I walk through it every day to get to my office. I do fabric presentations in the garden. It's given my design a more Zen, relaxed spin; my design is simpler, less formal. I love gardens. They are an ever-changing art."

Schoos created one of his trademark Buddha head fountains that rests in a fish pond. "The plants are a mix of tropical and cut flowers," Cohen says. "There are goldfish, yellow and pink waterlilies, lavender water hyacinth, and water cabbage in the pond. The colors are white against the green and gray. In summer I go with fuchsia and yellow orchids."

The four elements that went into the garden were water ("I wanted a block of color that was green, not blue, to relate to the garden colors"); flowers ("I only planted flowers I could cut and use in the house"); scent (from flowers and incense); and music ("an important element for the Zen quality—the sound of music and water relate to each other"). Instead of typical garden furniture, Cohen had awning fabric printed in a Fortuny design for the chairs and found a 1920s iron table, Chinese red lacquered nesting tables, an old Persian rug, and a Balinese futon.

[NATIVε]

It wasn't too long ago that native grasses were being mowed under by lawns and annuals. Now when you stand at the edge of a cliff on John Greenlee's patch of paradise overlooking the Pacific Ocean, you are surrounded by swaying stands of ornamental grasses of all shapes and sizes and from all corners of the world. It is a majestic sight—grasses waving in the strong breeze, surfers, and seals and dolphins offshore—that is both visually stunning and mentally invigorating.

Greelee's epiphany happened at the Western Hills Nursery in Occidental, California, where Marshall Olbrich and Lester Hawkins were introducing ornamental grasslands to the West Coast. Greenlee remembers walking through fields of natural grasses swaying in the breeze just when he was working on a house in San Marino. It was a modern house on one acre, and he and his then-partner Mike Sullivan decided to make the grounds look like something out of Pasadena three hundred years ago—all oak trees, savannah, and grasses. That first major job, in 1984, established Greenlee's reputation in the plant community. Greenlee then decided to go to the source. He went to work with Kurt Bluemel in Baltimore, Maryland, the king of ornamental grasses, and in 1987 he brought back a truckload of grasses to establish his own nursery in Pomona, California. In 1990 Greenlee published *Encyclopedia of Ornamental Grasses*, and he has since joined the growing ranks of nurserymen and landscapers who are ripping out big expanses of lawn and replacing them with tapestries of ornamental grasses woven together.

Then Greenlee met Robert Fletcher, a brilliant landscape architect who was the yin to Greenlee's yang. Fletcher taught landscape design at University of California Los Angeles in the 1980s and was a huge influ-

Perched on a bluff overlooking the Pacific Ocean, a sea of ornamental grasses and tree aloes sway in the breeze. John Greenlee, with the late landscape designer Robert Fletcher, planted the site for a client who allows him the use of his land in return for taking care of his rare collection of aloe and succulents.

ence on the Los Angeles garden scene. "Bob was the hotshot designer; I was the hotshot plantsman," recalls Greenlee, who studied horticulture at California Polytechnic in Pomona. The pair made a deal with their client, Charles Hagen, who owned the four magical acres in Malibu: they would maintain his substantial aloe and succulent collection; in return, they would have the use of his vacant parcel on a cliffside bluff.

Slowly they began to transform the land, one of the largest oceanfront parcels in Malibu. The planting began a chess match: Greenlee would drop off the plants and by the time he returned Fletcher would have made his move. It became a game of one-upmanship between the designer and the plantsman, but Greenlee learned some valuable lessons about planning outdoor rooms. "Bob put in the road and path system," says Greenlee. "I was prepared to lay everything out in straight rows. He made garden rooms with tall grasses. He was the one who taught me how to look at perspective and depth in a garden."

The perimeter is planted with giant eucalyptus and ficus meant to mimic the old hedges in Oxnard, California. Winding paths lead down past mini-meadows brimming with over 150 species of grass for every climate condition—sun, shade, wet, and dry—including *miscanthus* (Eulalia grass) from the Okavango Basin in Botswana, *manzanitas*,

ceanothus (wild lilac), *muhlenbergia* (an evergreen grass that attracts butterflies), and native sedge. Greenlee, who has started designing because he "grew tired of waiting for others to do it," uses the grass as a neutral design element and mixes it with succulents, redwoods, or coral trees. Before he died four years ago, Fletcher started planting in pairs, such as Monterey cypresses, and pepper trees.

The Malibu nursery has proved beneficial to business, since it was hard to get influential garden designers to trek inland to Pomona. "This is our Westside showroom, a place landscape designers can bring their clients," Greenlee says. Malibu has other benefits. At the beach, Greenlee gets to torture the plants with salt air and high winds before they are sent inland to bake in Pomona's heat and smog. That way he learns everything he needs to know about the grasses and how they will survive.

Greenlee's years of experimentation and his collaborations have humbled the former hotshot. "The more I learn, the more I know I'll never stop learning," he admits. "When you come out here in the late afternoon, the wind is rippling the grasses and they are in every color and texture—blue and red, creeping and cloudlike. Or it's a foggy day with misty beads of water and hummingbirds. This is a tangible place to bring people who become smitten, like I was smitten."

ABOVE AND OVERLEAF: Greenlee is at the forefront of the natural grass movement, a growing body of plantspeople who are bringing regional grasses back. He experiments with *manzanitas, muhlenbergia,* giant *miscanthus* ("that turns a pumpkin orange in the fall, when the wind strips the leaves and the leftover is a skeletal curtain"), and tapestries of fifteen succulents woven together.

What was once four acres of mustard grass five feet tall is now a testing area for an international array of 150 grasses from Chile, South America, North Africa, and New Zealand. About 60 percent are native and are meant for all climates and conditions—sun or shade, wet or dry. Greenlee, whose nursery is in Pomona, uses the Malibu site as a laboratory. "I get my coastal data from here and my inland data from Pomona," he says. "I get to torture the grasses with salt air and high wind before they are sent inland to bake in the heat and smog."

Pockets of "old" Los Angeles—downtown, Pasadena, Hancock Park—are studded with handsome turn-of-the-century Craftsman houses, the proud remnants of a golden age in California architecture. Typically set back from the street on deep lots, these houses epitomized the desire to turn a collective back on the Industrial Revolution and return to a handcrafted age. With a style that paid equal homage to the architecture of ancient Japan, the British Arts and Crafts movement, and Frank Lloyd Wright, the houses boasted gleaming wood paneling and beams, wide porches that provided the ideal perch for swings, and pergolas that extended the architecture of the house into the garden.

On a triple lot in Windsor Square, near Hancock Park, is an original Craftsman house. Scott and Lauren Goldstein purchased it in 1989 and were then given a golden opportunity to purchase the lot next door. "We bought the lot and tore down the tract house that had been built on it," says Scott, who produces films and documentaries.

The extra lot allowed them to indulge their passion for gardening. They dedicated the larger front portion as a garden and built a Craftsman-style guesthouse in the back. And along the way, these two New Yorkers took a surprising path. Instead of going country English, which was Lauren's inclination, they went native Californian. Everything planted relates to old California. To enter the garden is like taking a step back into another time, when chaparral, grasses, shrubs, and native oaks still ruled.

Part of the Goldsteins' decision was dictated by the earth itself—a hardpan layer of clay called caliche that is impossible to garden. So their first task was to surround the perimeter with raised beds filled with native soil. Since trees were going be the garden's central focus, they prepped the ground by digging huge holes six to seven feet deep, removed

A native Californian garden at Scott and Lauren Goldstein's house is full of toyons (the holly tree that used to cover the Hollywood hills), native oaks (scrub, Engelmann, island), pines, redwood, and willow trees underplanted with redbuds, salvia, artemisia, and poppies.

the clay, augered holes, and filled them with gravel—in effect, creating giant pots in the ground.

In the meantime, Scott had done vast amounts of research on climate, soil, native plants, companion plants, and under-plantings, and he stumbled across an entire subculture of native plant nurseries and growers. "Everyone thinks that southern California is naturally a desert, but it's not," he says. "It's dry coastal plain." They put in "hardpan penetrators"—native oaks, toyons (holly trees that used to cover the Hollywood hills), and certain pines. The raised beds were organized into plant communities that relate to the coast, foothills, or desert. "From a botanical point of view, it's better to choose biologically rather than aesthetically," he says.

Goldstein found a mother lode of mature trees next to a nursery in Claremont—an open site that was covered in chaparral. There he tagged a scrub oak, an Engelmann oak, an island oak (tomentella, native to the Channel Islands) that's now a gangly adolescent, a couple of redwoods, and a Spanish scrub oak that reminded the Goldsteins of the Basque country. Redbuds, *artemisia* (sagebrush), salvia, and matilija poppies give fragrance and color. A desert willow is one of the few trees that flowers all summer. "It's really a spring garden," Scott says. "In August it's in dormancy. By October it looks really stressed. But it's beautiful in any season."

There are thirty-six zones of irrigation via microsprays—miniature sprinklers that ensure that water only gets under the foliage. "You don't want the leaves to get wet, just the

soil," says Scott. "Native plants are prone to rot." Meandering circular paths lead around the front garden. Interspersed among the trees and shrubs are structured niches for swings, bowers, and fountains. From the Old Hickory Furniture Company's catalog, they ordered swings, seats, and rustic gates. A Batchelder fountain is reproduction tile made by a company called the Tile Restoration Center in Washington State.

A wood bower marks the transition from the front garden into the middle meadow, which was planted by John Greenlee (see p. 140), a major proponent of native grasses. Greenlee planned a "fantastical California meadow" and filled it with two thousand plugs of Laguna Mountain and Santa Barbara dryland sedge (it will grow in sun or shade, with or without water, and forms turf, making it, says Scott, the perfect lawn plant), mosquito grass, and California stipa (the state feather grass that used to grow on hillsides everywhere). The sweeping front lawn is buffalo grass. "Neighbors have noticed how well the native grasses work," says Lauren, who writes a gardening column for the local newspaper, *The Larchmont Chronicle*. "We are starting to spread the word."

Instead of buying a place in the country, the garden has become the family's hideaway in the city. "The garden quenched our manifest destiny," says Lauren.

Interspersed along the circular path are resting points and niches. A fountain made of reproduction Batchelder tile complements the couple's turn-of-the-century Craftsman house.

The furniture—a swing set, chairs and tables, a rustic bower—all came from the Old Hickory Company catalog. The garden has thirty-six zones of irrigation for controlling the rot that can plague native plants. In the center of the property is a meadow where John Greenlee has planted stipa, dryland sedge, and mosquito grass that is mowed once a year.

When Wesley and Marla Strick first saw their 1938 house in the Hollywood Hills, they were dirt poor, and living in New York, and didn't even own a car. But they fell in love with it anyway, and jokingly referred to it as "our house."

The fact that it had been Jack LaLanne's home for some thirty-five years and that it was where he raised his family only added to its appeal. The godfather of physical fitness had moved on, but the house was still in its full-blown LaLanne mode—statuary of Jack outside, fifty-five flecked mirrors, and flocked wallpaper inside. "It was hysterical," says Marla. "It looked like a Vegas brothel." But they loved it anyway, and whenever they stayed with friends in the neighborhood, they would drive by and visit "their house."

Along the way, Wesley Strick became a well-regarded screenwriter (*Final Analysis*, the *Cape Fear* remake, *Mission: Impossible 2*), and the Stricks moved up in the world and out to Los Angeles. And, this being Hollywood, the next time the family drove by the house, it had a For Sale sign. They bought the house the next day and have spent the past twelve years fixing it and the garden up.

The Stricks modernized the house with additions by the late architect Frank Israel and his partners Stephen Shortridge and Barbara Callas, and redesigned the pool. Marla Strick, a former antiques dealer and an impassioned gardener, instantly planned a tropical succulent garden around Southern California's climate. "I'm not a leafy person," she says. "I don't like bushy East Coast plants. I like things to be clean and readable, sculptural and riotous." She found a kindred spirit in Matthew Brown, who had just returned to Los Angeles after a long sojourn in Costa Rica and Oaxaca, Mexico, and was launching his own landscape design practice.

"I'm not a leafy person," says Marla Strick. "I like things to be clean and readable, sculptural and riotous." She and her husband, screenwriter Wesley Strick, have gradually taken Jack LaLanne's former house into the future with architectural additions, and back to the past with a garden of unusual native succulents.

The original garden had good bones. But "it was your typical concrete pool and flagstone patio with ivy and azaleas—the same old song and dance," Brown says. And it hadn't been maintained, so his task became more about editing, organizing, and changing it around to make it shine. "We deconstructed the flagstone to soften it—it was all square and hard," says Marla, who put in her own touches—a psychedelic chair and a stairway to nowhere. "Every window has a different view, so we were planting from the inside," she adds. "From the dining room, it's like looking at a painting. From the bedroom, we look down on the carob trees."

Marla and Brown both love rescuing other people's cast-off plants from dumps or abandoned sites. They put at least seventy species of succulents in the front garden—huge variegated agave, ocotillo, and yucca—some of which were cuttings given by friends. "The succulents look like they could be at the bottom of the ocean, like alien beings on another planet," says Marla. "I love the sparse shadow play against the walls." Pups from succulents fed other parts of the garden. They went shopping at quarries for unusual rocks. "I do everything slowly so that we can make mistakes," she adds.

"Most of my clients are young and are in the film or music business," says Brown, who grew up in Los Angeles and was a fan of Jack LaLanne. "They work hard and are harried. I give them a place to contemplate, where they can look at a couple of plants, concentrate on the texture and form and beauty, and let the day roll away." Brown calls his designs "strange and interesting, not pretty." The Strick garden is his most accessible, most easily understood project to date. "Gardens don't have to be about plants," he says. "There are no rules in Southern California."

LEFT: With a state park as the backdrop, Strick and landscape designer Matthew Brown put in desert and tropical plants "from cuttings from friends or from rescued strange plant material that we found abandoned in the trash," she says. *OPPOSITE:* Agave and aloe thrive in front of the new kitchen designed by the late Los Angeles architect Frank Israel.

ABOVE LEFT AND RIGHT: Marla Strick added her own idiosyncratic touches—a psychedelic bench and a stairway to nowhere—and rocks from local quarries. "I love the shadow play on the walls," she says of the succulents. *OPPOSITE:* "The lawn is for our kids."

[*HOLLYWOOD*]

Art Luna's life revolves around Sunset Plaza, a chic stretch of outdoor cafés and boutiques at the intersection of Sunset Boulevard and Sunset Plaza Drive in Los Angeles. His house is up a hill, just a two-minute ride from the boulevard. His beauty salon is five minutes from his house. One feeds the other—one "saves the other"—he says. A couple of years ago, after Luna replanted the salon's courtyards and some of his clients (Stockard Channing, Steve and Jamie Tisch, Ben Stiller) started asking him to do their gardens, he began to spend as much time on landscape design as on hair.

His own garden is, naturally, a work in constant progress. He is fine-tuning the hardscape—the outer brick terrace where flower beds and pots and pool come together—to make it lush. And he is replanting the softscape. But mostly he is trying to connect the gracious 1936 Mediterranean house to a lower, sloping lot. He is creating a flow and secret rooms that will make people want to experience it. He wants guests to be inside the garden, not just looking at it from above. He wants to lure people into all its hidden nooks and crannies, all its varied seating areas. "I want them to move, I want them to walk down there, I want them to enjoy it," Luna says.

He calls it a tropical garden with an English structure. And structure is his obsession. As structure underlies a great haircut, so structure underlies a great garden. He learned about structure in gardens from repeated visits to England's most admired estates (Sissinghurst, Hidcote, Great Dixter, Alderley Grange) and to friends' country houses in the Cotswolds. He read garden books voraciously—Russell Page's *Education of a Gardener*, and the writings of Anna Pavord, Gertrude Jekyll, Vita

Playing off the elegant lines of a 1936 Spanish Colonial house above Sunset Boulevard, Art Luna is making a lush garden that is part Far Eastern, part southern Californian, with some English structure thrown in for good bones. Structure is critical to the hairdresser-turned-landscape designer. Phoenix palms, giant bromeliads, and sago palms act as the terrace's railing, delineating the edge without blocking the view. "I like architecture in plants," he says.

Sackville-West, and Lawrence Johnston. "I'm drawn to gardeners who aren't formally trained," Luna says. "Gertrude Jekyll knew about plants from art and studying the old Dutch masters."

Lotusland in Santa Barbara showed him how a sense of age could be conveyed through mass plantings of agave and aloes. He researched what worked best and put in trees (jacaranda, Norfolk pines, *Eugenia*) that flourished on neighboring lots. "Know your zone" is his mantra. A long lane of double-white datura (angel's trumpet) underplanted with gardenias leads to a putting green (the legacy of a former owner). Above and below the putting green, he is regrading the slope. Out came nine hundred lily bulbs and in came terraces and box hedges. "Clearing and leveling" is how Luna describes his transformation of the lower garden. "It's organized and well planned now," Luna says. "As soon as I figured it out, it felt right and peaceful."

Living above Sunset is, for Art Luna, a very urban experience, the equivalent to living on Park Avenue. His connection to the city is immediate—the sounds of car alarms, sirens, and horns from Sunset, directly below, coupled with a dead-on view of the city. "I've had to make peace with the fact that it's a city garden and that it's not quiet," says Luna. His partner, interior designer Tim Clarke, worries that Luna is taking the view away bit by bit. In truth, Luna doesn't like the view much. He finds it overwhelming and, on smoggy days, depressing. And he wants the garden to have height, and for that he needs trees.

But he has created quiet zones. To the side of the house is a narrow strip where he placed a large Buddha fountain from Thomas Schoos that set the whole garden in motion. It was too large for its spot, so Luna started making it less of a showpiece and more a part of the garden, adding in more green with mounds of ferns in pots, putting a staghorn fern above, planting giant timber and Mexican and weeping bamboo and maple, and making it less Zen/Japanese and more Far Eastern. A far back corner that was wasted space is now more cavelike and "beautiful creepy," with black bamboo, white orchids, clematis, and philodendron. A row of sago palms outside the living room acts as a wall and breaks up the view from the terrace to the pool without blocking it. Grey and terra-cotta Bauer pots and tree-stump pots from 1919 hold giant bromeliads, Phoenix palms, and topiary gardenias. "I like what other people have, but the garden has to be mine," says Luna, who seeks out the unusual and exotic, such as *synadenium*, Dutchman's pipe, and ficuses with triangular leaves.

"The quiet subtleties of a garden make you remember it," he adds. "Landscaping is a soulful, heartfelt thing—you get to see your plants looking healthy. At work I get to handle beauty. Here I get to create it."

"Clearing and leveling" made the lower lot "seem right and peaceful," says Luna. Box hedges give structure to the lower lawn, the only level land and a swath of solid green that Luna intends to keep. The plants relate to what does well around him: Norfolk pines, jacarandas, Eugenia ("I love it—it is old California," says Luna who grew up in Southern California).

Rows of French doors open onto to the back terrace and pool. "I had to figure out how to make the garden on hardscape (brick and tile) feel lush," says Luna, who juggles what goes in the flowerbeds and what goes into pots. He and Tim Clarke entertain outdoors a lot—as gardener and interior designer, their house is their showroom. "People love the garden as much as us—it is an extension of the house." The feeling of scale and height is achieved with the plants in pots. A visit to Lotusland showed him how to use agave and succulents to convey a sense of age.

The original 1930s tiled swimming pool "gives a sense of color" against a solid hedge of Eugenia. All the pots are either gray terra-cotta Bauer or tree-stump pots from 1919.

A Buddha head from Thomas Schoos started Luna on the garden journey two years ago. It dwarfed its side space, so he started to plant around it—with a staghorn fern, maples, moss, mounds of ferns in pots, and timber bamboo. "It feels like a secret garden in here, like you can sit and hide from the pool," says Luna.

Erin Lareau works with glass—pavé crystal, to be precise. She takes a computer mouse or an old movie camera or a globe and covers it with a multitude of tiny colored crystals until it sparkles. "By transforming the antiquated and the mundane into *objets de fantasie*, I create totems that honor my dreams of living the life of a princess," she once wrote.

Lareau and her husband bought their 1961 Hollywood Hills house mainly for its half-acre of level garden—unusual for the hills. "The great gift was that the big expensive plants were put in when the house was built—the hedges, palm trees, and a giant bird of paradise," says Lareau. "But it was a bit *Sanford and Son*. The lawn was dirt and the house was a disaster. We didn't realize how nice it was until we remodeled it."

Lareau plunged into fixing up the garden, even though she admits that she knew nothing about gardening. "Agapanthus and geraniums are the only plants I grew up with," she says. "I've been a gypsy all my life." So she went to the Huntington and Descanso Gardens and she got the *Los Angeles Times* garden books by Robert Smaus and Sunset's *Western Garden Book* out of the library. As she learned plant names, a new world opened up. Her first decisions were to put in a xeriscape garden with succulents. "We did the planting in one big swoop because we were married in the garden about eight months after we moved in," she says. "I registered at Mordigan Nurseries for our wedding—it was the best idea I ever had."

But the wood walkway that ran straight down the middle of the lawn was still an eyesore. "It was rotten and pretty dangerous," Lareau says. She thought about using tinted cement, but then she was flipping through a magazine and saw a glass garden by Andrew Cao. "I work with glass; I'm absolutely mad for glass."

Curved paths of glass undulate around a circular pond where Miss Diva Thing reigns. Glass artist Erin Lareau's sculpture is glass on glass on glass—pavé glass on fiberglass standing on recycled glass pebbles. Datura drips its angel trumpets—"it has a fantastic scent," says Lareau.

ABOVE: "I created her for the garden," says Lareau of her glass sculpture. "Her curves match the beds. We even have curved furniture to soften the angularity of the house." Glass landscaper Andy Cao made the pond and pedestal for Miss Diva Thing, then Lareau filled in with Queen of Siam waterlilies.
OPPOSITE: "Everything is about design, symmetry, and color." The "big expensive plants"—palms, giant bird of paradise, hedges—were already in place when she bought the house.

Lareau immediately called Cao, and she became one of the first residential clients of this now-renowned young garden designer, who takes old wine bottles, marbles or industrial glass and recycles them into sparkling glass gardenscapes, glass tile, and even glass cobblestones. "Andy came out to talk about the walkway, and the project grew," she says. "The house is all angular but I was dying for curves." The walkway ended up curved, so the side beds became curved, and Cao created a glass moat around the palm trees. "Andy loved my glass work, so he made a pond and put Miss Diva Thing, one of my pieces, on a pedestal in the middle. Now I have pavé glass on top of fiberglass sitting on recycled glass—it's all about glass." At night, the glass walkway looks like a river running through the garden.

And while pavé glass is Lareau's true medium, she uses the garden as a canvas. "I pay a lot of attention to color. The colors are all pink, yellow, green, and blue, but they are saturated pastels—hot pink, sage green, and aquamarine."

With all the basic elements in place, Lareau felt free to finally fulfill one fantasy. "We built up the original rose garden, and then I began to indulge my love of tulips," she says. "I buy a couple of crates every fall and plant them and have a big slew of tulips in spring. It's an indulgence, but I can't help myself. In spring I have an English garden of tulips and daffodils; in summer, it's all roses and angel trumpets."

The former professional dancer and costume designer is content with her career and her house. "I'm set now," Lareau says. "I plan to be here in my compound until I'm 105. The garden led me to the house, and my love for the garden opened my mind to the house; by opening my mind, it expanded my taste and vision."

ABOVE: When Lareau and her husband married in their back garden, she registered at a local nursery. "It was the best idea I ever had." Her first task was putting in a succulent garden. *OPPOSITE:* "My favorite spot is on the porch swing," Lareau says. "I'm letting Boston ivy grow around the posts—it softens the loggia and it's nice to have strands hanging." She found the vintage garden furniture at a swap meet. "I can usually assemble a bouquet of flowers for dinner parties any time of year," says Lareau, who has night-blooming jasmine, apple-scented geraniums, agapanthus, roses, and orchids to choose from.

Duane Phay is emphatic about what he does and doesn't like. "I am very picky, very black and white," he says. "I'm not gray and I'm not wishy-washy." When he went house-hunting, he had a precise wish list—the house had to be on a promontory so that he didn't look into anyone else's bedroom, it had to have a view, it had to have a pool, and it had to be reasonably priced. To his surprise, he found it at the very top of a street above Los Angeles, with sweeping views from downtown to the ocean.

Phay is equally emphatic about creating a streamlined environment. While the bones of the house were good and it was beautifully sited, its whitewashed bricks and shag carpet had to go. Phay removed the bricks and red-tile roof, ripped out the brown shag carpet and dark wood paneling, and repainted the mustard ceilings; he brought in purpleheart wood floors and experimented with a stainless steel grid paneling on the walls. Now all is calm and minimalist, and every angle is framed for contrast and drama.

"I steal all my ideas from the movies," admits Phay, who was born and raised in Singapore and London and has spent his life living in different parts of the world, most recently Australia. Now that he has alighted in Los Angeles, he wants his house and garden to be of the city, but not to look like it. To his dismay, all the landscapers he talked to wanted to put in palm trees. "I didn't want the garden to look like I was in L.A.," he says.

Once he found landscape architect Russell Cletta, a partner of top Los Angeles landscaper Jay Griffith, they went to work, guided by Phay's vision. Phay's inspirations are a blur of architecture, movies and fashion: Le Corbusier's Villa Savoye, modern Swedish design, Oscar Niemeyer's buildings in Brazil, Villa Malaparte, John Galliano gowns, and *Mommie Dearest*.

Apart from the pool inside the front gate with a concrete deck, all that existed were hills of ivy. There was no outdoor space. They constructed a

From the top of a hill, Duane Phay has juxtaposed a tight symmetry of a sliding door, which came from Disney World's Tomorrow Land, and a tiled water channel with sprawling views of the city.

cantilevered outdoor terrace on the slope outside the living room. Ficus trees planted on the hillside had to be hoisted in by crane. Phay keeps the ficus trimmed, forcing them lower and lower, training them to be his "lawn." Water now flows around the house, starting with a spout that trickles into the pool; then a narrow channel by the front door drops a wall of water over the side down into a spa that is lined in purple and blue tile from Brazil.

Every tiny detail was meticulously thought out and handcrafted. The stairs leading down to the deck, for example, are solid steel, but where they cross over the water, they become grates. The handrail is based on a design he saw in Sweden. The sliding Chinese-style modern screens at the front door came from DisneyWorld's Tomorrow Land, and they epitomize the past/future tense of the house.

Phay originally wanted gray, not green, plants in front. Spindly *melaleuca* trees (an Australian native) border the pool. Very few plant materials were used; everything is very pared down. "I hate warmth," Phay says. "I'm not afraid of color, but I wanted everything gray. Like my wardrobe, with its very limited color palette." He imagined the pool as a biblical scene from *The Ten Commandments,* and the plants as reeds. Two round pots were filled with succulents to look like bowls of candy.

From his perch, Phay can see the planes descending into LAX, the Getty Center, oil tankers offshore, and the sun shimmering on the ocean. It's an idealized picture of the city, and the perfect picture frame for an original spirit like Phay.

Phay admits that he steals all his design ideas from movies. *RIGHT:* He and landscape architect Russell Cletta installed a pared-down, gray garden with few plant materials. The impact is in the details: hibiscus in small bowls and round pots filled with succulents to look like bowls of candy. *OPPOSITE:* The water channel overflows and cascades down the side of the house to create a waterfall.

ABOVE: Inspired by a trip to Brazil, Phay used purple and blue Brazilian tile for the spa. The steps leading down to the deck go from solid at the top and bottom to grates over the water. *ABOVE RIGHT AND OPPOSITE:* "I hate warmth," says Phay. "I'm not afraid of color, but I wanted everything to be gray." To soften the wall around the front garden and pool, Cletta put in spindly Australian *melaleuca* trees and reeds. "It looks like it all comes from next to a river—like out of *The Ten Commandments,*" Phay says.

ABOVE: "There are no curves, except for the outside wall," says Phay. "The landscape softens everything." *OPPOSITE:* Phay built the cantilevered deck outside the living room and installed the round fire pit. At dusk, the fire is reflected in the glass panels. "It's all about contrast and drama," Phay says.

She grew up in Beverly Hills. She made fashion history with her first film. She spent a decade as a costume designer, then gave up one of the top careers in Hollywood to move to Northern California to run a bed-and-breakfast. Fifteen years ago Theadora van Runkle returned to her house atop Laurel Canyon. It is her beloved place, and she thinks she will probably die there.

Van Runkle's reputation was secured overnight with her outfits for *Bonnie and Clyde* (1967), which were instantly copied around the globe. Even today, top fashion designers pay homage to her influence. The inspiration for Faye Dunaway's costumes? The dresses in Jean Cocteau's screen fable *Beauty and the Beast*. "*Beauty and the Beast* informed everything I've done," says Van Runkle. "The bodices on Beauty's costumes—the scrubbing dresses more than the court gowns—influenced everything in Faye's costumes: the shape of the ribcage in relationship to the waist and the shirts dropped down a couple of inches so that you could see the hip bone."

Beauty and the Beast also informed her garden, a wondrous fantasy in black and green that is framed by massive trellises. Like the scaffolding on a stage set, the trellises rise around the garden, as both visual impact and as a practical place to hang plants and chandeliers, mirrors and crystals.

Van Runkle bought her house in the mid-1960s and rented it out to a procession of tenants. The cottage is tiny, almost swallowed up by the gardens, but everything is painted white and it is elegantly and simply furnished. Mementos from her Hollywood days abound, including a table owned by Jeanette MacDonald and the bed from *Wuthering Heights*. There is even a souvenir of her time in Mendocino, albeit a rather large one. Adjacent to the cottage is a round, two-story tower where she does

"I've always responded to damp, glistening leaves, to things that grow in the shade," says Theadora van Runkle. The costume designer (*Bonnie and Clyde, Bullitt, The Thomas Crown Affair*) has owned her Hollywood Hills cottage since the 1960s and has put her movie magic to work on its gardens. "I like to lie on the couch and read or write poetry," she says, "but it's rare for a gardener to have time to sit down."

most of her painting and where she is cataloging her archive of sketches and paintings. The tower started life as a 280,000-gallon Beaujolais wine vat for Sebastiani Brothers. It is made of redwood, dates from 1860, and was transported down in sections.

The house follows the spiral path of an argonaut shell. It's the same pattern, van Runkle notes, that architect Stanford White used to make his houses more habitable. The garden is structured and voluptuous at the same time. A gravel walkway strewn with glass pebbles that she hurls around in handfuls leads from the front gates straight to the cottage. But along the way are numerous nooks furnished with chairs, tables, and couches, providing resting spots depending on whether she wants to paint, read, write poetry, or eat outside.

Towering pines and elms filter the sunlight and heighten the dramatic effect. "I like the Provençal climate where things are seared by the sun," van Runkle says in amusement. "So I'm not sure how I ended up with no soil and no sun. But I've always responded to damp, glistening leaves and things that grow in the shade. I adored the ferns and ferny grottoes in the High Sierra that I saw as a child." Other childhood influences bubble to the garden's surface. "I was closest to my mother when we went to nurseries or to Chinatown for dinner and we'd see Amazon lilies in storefronts or on tables," she says. "I associate the exoticism of the East with shade."

Like *Beauty and the Beast*, the garden is a magical, mystical place. "This little ledge is a force field of some sort," van Runkle says. "Each plant sends off its own resonance." Her passion is begonias, planted tall in black urns that are mounted on plinths and pedestals and form a stately procession down the walkway. Antique garden statuary, Buddhas and sphinxes are carefully interspersed.

When van Runkle was a child, she saw a watercolor of rex begonias by the fashion illustrator René Boucher, and that image has guided her garden. Rudi Zeizenpenne, a ninety-nine-year-old man in Santa Barbara, has been her longtime begonia supplier and teacher. "He is a propogation expert and the greatest botanist I know," she says. Rapacious begonias sprout massive leaves and white, ladylike blossoms. Ferns grow giant here, too. "Each one wants to be the biggest," she says. "Each one speaks to me."

Her plants are her children, and like children they are named, talked to and nurtured. She's had Gunga, her star begonia, for thirty years. One giant orchid, with leaves that dangle four feet, is also thirty years old. Cornelia Carbentus is a fern named after van Gogh's mother, who was, she notes, "a good watercolorist in her own right."

Van Runkle belongs to the last generation of Hollywood's Golden Age, a period when costume designers created all the outfits for a movie and oversaw teams of seamstresses. She had an unlimited budget and was driven around town in a chauffeured car—her driver would carry her bag when she shopped for fabrics, so that when she put it down she wouldn't forget it. Then she dropped out of the Hollywood scene to move north with her second husband and her children; by the time she came back in the mid-1980s, the film industry had changed.

The one constant in her life has been her house and garden. "The house has been my little helping friend," van Runkle reflects. "Churchill said, 'We buy our houses, and our houses determine our lives.' Who would have thought that this small unassuming cottage and its garden would have determined my life?"

Rex begonias, ferns, and orchids are van Runkle's passion, and she has owned some of her plants for thirty years. Shaded by ash tree, Italian stone pine, and eucalyptus, her garden is dark and fertile, with each plant battling it out to be the biggest. "This little ledge is a force field of some sort," she says. "Each plant sends off its own resonance."

Like the set from *Beauty and the Beast,* Jean Cocteau's classic film interpretation of the fairy tale, the garden is framed by green trellis, chandeliers dangle from tree branches, and the gravel path is strewn with glass pebbles that she "hurls around in handfuls." Antique statuary and urns give each seating area a focal point.

"It's a small, unassuming cottage, but I have been very happy here and the garden has determined my life," van Runkle says. "Scale and contrast are important—white flowers against dark shadows. But it's mostly a green garden with green wicker garden furniture."

The porch outside her cottage holds her beloved begonias, anthurium, and polypodium ferns with some Oriental antiques mixed in. These days van Runkle, who started her career doing fashion illustrations, is painting and is cataloguing her archives of costume sketches and drawings from her films. "There's nothing like movie magic," she says.

Dawnridge is the ultimate Los Angeles stage set. It is part garden and part backdrop, where nothing is at is seems. It is at once real and ethereal, otherworldly and everyday, draped at the intersection of reality and fantasy. From his perch—high on a narrow ridge above Beverly Hills, facing east—Tony Duquette lived in a world completely of his own invention.

He and his wife Elizabeth, whom he nicknamed Beegle (because she had "the industry of a bee and the soaring poetry of an eagle"), divided their time between Los Angeles and San Francisco, with frequent sorties to Europe and Asia. But Hollywood was a constant presence in the lives of the two artists. They were married in 1949 at nearby Pickfair—Mary Pickford was the maid of honor and her second husband, Buddy Rogers, was the best man.

The Duquettes purchased their land from Cobina Wright, a Hearst columnist, for fifteen hundred dollars in 1949, and they got three-and-a-half lots overlooking a ravine originally called Fiddler's Ditch. No one in Los Angeles was better suited to turn the everyday into the fantastic, the ordinary into the magical. Tony Duquette had trained with top Los Angeles interior designers William Haines and James Pendleton. He had dressed shop windows for Bullock's and Robinson's; he had created costumes for the original Broadway production of *Camelot* and film sets for *Kismet* and *The Ziegfeld Follies*; he designed jewelry for Bergdorf Goodman; and he conjured interiors for clients around the globe.

Dawnridge was his headquarters and laboratory, and it was where guests and clients could see Duquette's vision in action. "My design work may appear opulent and luxurious," he wrote in *Architectural Digest* in March 1978, "yet for me the magical element consists in the juxtaposing of

Pagodas, pavilions, spirit houses, and miniature worlds were what Tony Duquette adored and conjured up at Dawnridge, his exuberant wonderland in Beverly Hills that has been kept intact by his longtime business partner, Hutton Wilkinson.

Duquette was a designer of sets, jewelry, furniture, and interiors, and Dawnridge gave him an exotic backdrop for his objects made of everyday materials. *ABOVE LEFT:* An eight-foot-tall sculpture of resin, which he made to look like alabaster. *ABOVE RIGHT: The Phoenix Rising from His Flames,* one of his assemblages, was made after a fire in his San Francisco studio destroyed a set of angel sculptures. *OPPOSITE:* The garden is a series of terraces and outdoor rooms that descend into the ravine.

works of art with the wonderful works of nature: shells, coral, the patterned skins of lizards, the bones of fish and animals."

From the street, there is no hint of the magic: all that is visible is a long gray exterior wall covered in trellises and vines. Inside, every door feels as though it will lead you into another world. The interiors are a theatrical and lavish concoction of paintings, Oriental rugs, Chinese wallpaper, mirrors, Fortuny fabrics, and intricately carved furniture. "I love gold and rich fabrics," he wrote in 1978, "but, like the Greek peasant who cannot gild his icon and so makes an exquisite one out of gold paper, I work equally with burlap and velvet. Beauty, not luxury, is what I value."

The gardens, which descend in a series of terraces and bridges fifty feet down the ravine, were designed, like the house, as one secret enclosed room unfolding into another. From the 1960s until his death in 1999, Duquette used gardening as his therapy. He was a master conjurer, the canniest of street scavengers. Some of the plants he put in were recycled from Chavez Ravine when Dodger Stadium was built. Jade, yucca, agave and succulents were appropriated from neighboring Beverly Hills estates. Even when dressed in a tux and headed for a movie premiere, Duquette would think nothing of pulling the car over if he saw something interesting—objects, plants—sticking out of a garbage can.

His soaring sunburst mirrors, his eight-foot-tall "jewels" that dangle from pagodas and pavilions, and the dazzling outdoor sculptures are, upon close inspection, constructed of street reflectors, hubcaps, and even skateboards. Plastic grates were painted green and mounted on walls like Chinese fretwork. Tall fruit pickers became lamp holders. Pillars are street lights. Duquette, says his longtime business partner Hutton Wilkinson, was a regular at Army and Navy sales, snapping up old tires and airplane parts, and anything else that had texture.

Duquette traveled frequently to Bali, and the influence shows. "The garden looks like a Balinese rain forest when it rains, like a tropical jungle," says Wilkinson. The grounds are populated with spirit houses, pagodas, and pavilions. He loved what he called "the natural baroque"—the ornate structure and curves found in animal skeletons or seashells. He loved bugs and frogs and abalone.

"He wasn't interested in one perfect rose or lawn," says Wilkinson. Duquette wanted abundance and lushness. He was first and foremost an artist (he had studied at the Chouinard Art Institute in Los Angeles), and in his garden he painted with light and with different shades of green, and with striped and variegated leaves. Everything was put into pots so that he could move plants around. Tree branches were painted coral to look like coral. He even insisted on watering the plastic plants.

Towering majestically in the middle of the garden is *The Phoenix Rising from His Flames*. It is one of a series of cast-resin assemblages of found objects that Duquette created after a 1989 fire destroyed a series of angels he had made for the city

"My design work, whether in jewelry or mandalas, interiors of Irish castles or beach houses, may appear opulent and luxurious, yet for me the magical element consists in the juxtaposing works of art with the wonderful works of nature," Duquette wrote. "He wasn't interested in one perfect rose," says Wilkinson. "He wanted abundance and lushness." Duquette painted with light and with different shades of green, and striped and variegated leaves.

of Los Angeles. Fire was a constant in Duquette's life. The very first fire, nicknamed Krakatoa, claimed the rental house below Dawnridge, but it also gave him the garden. His Malibu ranch, Sortilegium ("Enchantment"), was destroyed by fire in 1993. The phoenix became an appropriate symbol. Duquette believed that birds symbolized people, and he likened himself to the phoenix, "the bird that bridges a gap between two worlds," he wrote. "One world is nature in all her guises—mineral, vegetable, animal, earth, air, fire, water. The other is half unreal, dimly seen, magical, fantastic, the stuff of old stories, the dimension beyond the human spirit."

Dawnridge became what he called a "celebrational environment." Meals were taken on a shaded terrace next to the house that overlooks the gardens. Multiple decks extended the spaces out and gave different viewing platforms and perspectives. At the bottom of the ravine, reached by a series of wood stairs and bridges, is Beegle's painting studio (she did the paintings for Elizabeth Taylor in *The Sandpiper*) and a caretaker's house. A koi pond is fringed by bamboo and spider ferns.

Beegle died in 1996, and Duquette three years later, and a lifetime of belongings were auctioned by Christie's in Los Angeles. But Dawnridge is still filled to the rafters with the objects that were made specifically for the house and Wilkinson still welcomes an endless procession of acolytes. And the garden still stands as a monument to a man who celebrated the inner child until he died at age eighty-five. "My life has been involved with the constant effort of projecting a 'dimension beyond,'" Tony Duquette wrote. "Of releasing whatever magic, surprise, or treasured memory is held by a fabric, painting, or piece of antique or modern furniture."

Ferns drape from the outdoor dining terrace over the pool, which is encrusted with shells. "Design as applied to a dwelling means, for me, the creation of a magical ambiance that is greater than the sum of its parts," Duquette wrote. "The residence that I share with my artist wife, Elizabeth, is an expression of this credo."

"The garden looks like a Balinese rain forest when it rains, like a tropical jungle," says Hutton Wilkinson, who inherited the house and continues the design practice. Duquette could take the everyday and turn it into the extraordinary. His garden at Dawnridge is the epitome of Hollywood—a glimpse into a world that is glamorous, breathtaking, magical and unreal.

ERICA LENNARD

It is November and I am driving from Hollywood to Pacific Palisades on Sunset Boulevard. I have just returned from New York where it is cold, wet, and gray. Los Angeles is intoxicatingly warm, with not even a hint of fall in the air. As I pass by house after house, I try to catch glimpses of hidden-away gardens; I've learned that great treasures can often be found.

I was raised in New York and San Francisco, but fell in love with gardens when I moved to Paris to begin my photography career. That was more than twenty-five years ago. This love affair has taken me to some of the most beautiful gardens in the world; it never occurred to me that I might one day come to live in Los Angeles—a city that is, in a sense, all about the garden.

It happened by chance. My husband, interior designer Denis Colomb, and I have a great friend, Laurie Frank, who lives in the Whitley Heights section of Hollywood Hills. This community, developed in the 1920s, was originally intended to be a neighborhood for movie stars; it was one of the first. Maurice Chevalier was a previous owner of Laurie's house.

Whenever we visited Laurie from icy Paris or frigid New York we would pay a call on her neighbor-friends, French actor Patrick Bauchau, known to us from his films with Wim Wenders and Eric Rohmer, and his wife Mijanou Bardot, sister of the legendary Brigitte. When we arrived at their house, we would invariably find this beautiful couple sipping tea in the courtyard of their wonderful and mysterious Mediterranean-style home. We almost never went inside the house. We sat outside, surrounded by fruit trees of every type—avocado, fig, grapefruit, guava, lemon, mango, pomegranate, and olive—as well as bamboo, cacti, datura, jasmine, lavender, magnolias, passionflowers, rosemary, roses, and much more.

When Lennard and her husband, Denis Colomb, first visited Patrick and Mijanou's Hollywood garden, they left wondering why anyone would want to live anywhere else, without ever imagining that one day they would live there themselves.

Patrick spent ten years transforming the hillside, which was covered in dead ivy but had a few trees (notably the avocado trees that attracted him to the property in the first place), into what he describes as partly monastic (a product of growing up in a home with a Renaissance-style garden) and partly just plain wild, with plants that were chosen for no real rhyme or reason other than that they reminded him of the seasons. His goal was to create a private oasis that he and his wife could enjoy, and, as he would point out, gardening gave him something to do in between projects.

Each time my husband and I left their garden we would wonder why on earth we were living anywhere else. But never in a million years would we have thought that we'd be living in their house someday—a house where once-legendary Louise Brooks and later, rumor has it, George Saunders and Bette Davis, lived.

I remember the thought I had when we arrived at the house on that day in January when we moved in: we could be outside in a garden, or look outside into it, all the time. The feeling of euphoria was overwhelming. The days were richer and more meaningful than I had ever experienced while living in any other city. Our last apartment in Paris overlooked the majestic Tuileries gardens, which was why we took the place, but there were never any private moments to be had: we could only observe its magnificence. When we first moved into our house in Los Angeles, I had to keep reminding myself that the garden was real and not a stage set. It was filled with plants I had never seen before, and I ran out to buy Sunset's *Western Garden Book*.

The garden is wild and makes no sense sometimes, and, except for details, is very difficult to photograph. But it provides daily surprises, and it is because of this garden that I was inspired to find out about other people's sanctuaries—their secret gardens. I am not a gardener but an observer of gardens, and this is what I have attempted to share in this volume.

Patrick's garden creation is all in the details. Rare plants and poetic inscriptions abound in this fantasy world, where Lennard and Colomb feel privileged to spend their days.

BARBARA DRAKE
Garden of Eva, 562-428-7252 and 323-461-6556.
Worldwide Exotics, 818-890-1915, or at the Hollywood Farmer's Market every Sunday.

LAURA MORTON AND JEFF DUNAS
Laura Morton, 310-659-9046, www.lauramortondesign.com.

NANCY MEYERS
Mia Lehrer and Associates, 213-384-3844.

MARY STEENBURGEN AND TED DANSON
Susan Lindsey and Associates, 100 Barrington Walk, Suite A, Los Angeles, 310-476-5712.

LAURA COOPER AND NICK TAGGART
The Arboretum of Los Angeles County, 301 North Baldwin Avenue, Arcadia, 626-821-3222, www.arboretum.org.
Desert to Jungle Nursery, 3211 West Beverly Boulevard, Montebello, 323-722-3976.
Huntington Botanical Garden's succulent sales, 1151 Oxford Road, San Marino, 626-405-2100, www.huntington.org.
Pacific Horticulture magazine.

ANA ROTH
Filoli, Cañada Road, Woodside, 650-364-8300, www.filoli.org.
Nicky Nichols, 323-650-2967.
Sunset Boulevard Nursery, 4368 Sunset Boulevard, 323-661-1642.

ROLAND EMMERICH
James H. Cowan and Associates, Malibu, 310-457-2574.
Greenlee Nursery, Pomona, 909-629-9045.
Highland Succulents, Gallipolis, Ohio, 740-256-1428.
Susan McEowen, 661-294-3753.
San Marcos Growers, 805-683-1561, www.smgrowers.com.
Elizabeth Stevenson, 310-827-0323.

LATANA
Garett Carlson, LandArc, 10050 Reevesbury Drive, Beverly Hills, 310-858-7355.

JUDY HORTON
Judy M. Horton Garden Design, 323-462-1413.

CONNIE BUTLER AND DAVID SCHAFER
Judy Kameon, Elysian Landscapes, 323-226-9588, www.elysianlandscapes.com, www.plainair.com.

BARBARA HOWARD
Barry Sattels, 323-962-5565.

SUZANNE RHEINSTEIN
Hollyhock, 817 Hilldale, West Hollywood, 310-777-0100.
Judy M. Horton Garden Design, 323-462-1413.
Suzanne Rheinstein & Associates, 310-550-8900.
James Yoch, 405-321-6042.

SCOOTER AND MARILYN WILSON
Garett Carlson, LandArc, 10050 Reevesbury Drive, Beverly Hills, 310-858-7355.
Brian Diamond, Native Designs, 818-653-0513.
Exotic Garden Nursery, 18801 Victory Blvd., Reseda, 818-996-1684.
Green Thumb Nursery, 21812 Sherman Way, Canoga Park, 818-340-6400, www.supergarden.com.
Koan Collection, 6109 Melrose Avenue, Los Angeles, 213-464-3735, www.koan-collection.com.
Pusaka Collection, 1111 N. Crescent Heights Blvd., West Hollywood, 323-650-2952.
Sego, 12126 Burbank Boulevard, North Hollywood, 818-763-5711.
Thomas Schoos, 8618 Melrose Avenue, West Hollywood, 310-854-1141.
Warisan, 7470 Beverly Boulevard, Los Angeles, 323-938-3960, www.warisan.com.

LISA BITTAN
Acquisitions, 1020 South Robertson Boulevard, Los Angeles, 310-289-0196.

Desert Gardens by Melba Levick and Gary Lyons (Rizzoli, 2000).
Curt Klebaum, 310-413-1770.
Serra Gardens Landscape Succulents, 3314 Serra Road, Malibu, 310-456-1572.

SUSAN COHEN
Susan Cohen Associates, Santa Monica, 310-828-4445.
Dalsol Orchid Warehouse, 766 San Julian Street, Los Angeles, 213-614-1925.
Orchids de Oro, 3077 La Cienega Boulevard, Culver City, 310-838-4262.
Thomas Schoos, 8618 Melrose Avenue, West Hollywood, 310-854-1141.
David Tisherman, Manhattan Beach, 310-379-6700.

JOHN GREENLEE
Kurt Bluemel Nurseries, 2740 Greene Lane, Baldwin, Maryland, 800-498-1560, www.kurtbluemel.com.
Neil Diboll, Prairie Nursery, Westfield, Wisconsin, 608-296-3679.
Greenlee Nursery, 241 East Franklin Avenue, Pomona, 909-629-9045.
Western Hills Rare Plant Nursery, 16250 Coleman Valley Road, Occidental, 707-874-3731.

SCOTT GOLDSTEIN
Greenlee Nursery, 301 East Franklin Avenue, Pomona, 909-629-9045.
Las Pilitas, Santa Margarita, 805-438-5992.
Lummis Home State Historic Monument, 200 East Avenue 43, Los Angeles, 213-222-0546.
Rancho Santa Ana Botanic Garden, 1500 North College Avenue, Claremont, 909-625-8767.
Santa Barbara Botanic Garden, 1212 Mission Canyon Road, Santa Barbara, 805-682-4726.
Theodore Payne Foundation and Native Plant Nursery, 10459 Tuxford Street, Sun Valley, 818-768-1802 and 818-768-3533.
Tree of Life Nursery, 33201 Oretga Highway, San Juan Capistrano, 949-728-0685, www.treeoflifenursery.com.

WESLEY AND MARLA STRICK
Matthew Brown Landscape, 213-382-2994.
Serra Gardens Landscape Succulents, 3314 South Serra Road, Malibu, 310-456-1572.

ART LUNA
Inner Gardens, 6050 West Jefferson Boulevard, Culver City, 310-838-8378.
La Cienega Nursery, 8511 Sherwood Drive, Los Angeles, 310-659-5468.
Lotusland, 695 Ashley Road, Santa Barbara, 805-969-9990.
Art Luna, 8930 Keith Ave., West Hollywood, 310-247-1383.

ERIN LAREAU
Erin Lareau, 323-851-9444, www.erinlareau.com.
Andrew Cao, Landscape2go, Los Angeles, 213-368-9220, www.landscape2go.com.
Huntington Botanical Gardens, 1151 Oxford Road, San Marino, 626-405-2100, www.huntington.org.
Descanso Gardens, 1418 Descanso Drive, La Cañada, 818-949-4200, www.descanso.com.
Mordigan Nurseries, 7933 West Third Street, Los Angeles, 323-655-6027.

JONI MITCHELL
Cosetino's, 25019 Pacific Coast Highway, Malibu, 310-456-6026.
Oasis Imports, 3931 South Topanga Canyon (at Pacific Coast Highway), Malibu, 310-456-9883.

DUANE PHAY
Russell Cletta, Griffith & Cletta, 310-399-4727.

THEADORA VAN RUNKLE
Acquisitions, 1020 South Robertson Boulevard, Los Angeles, 310-289-0196.
La Cienega Nursery, 8511 Sherwood Drive, Los Angeles, 310-659-5468.
Mickey Hargitay Plants, 1255 North Sycamore Avenue, Hollywood, 323-467-8044, www.mickeysplants.com.